Die Ahnenstammkartei
des Deutschen Volkes

An

Introduction and Register

---

compiled by

Thomas Kent Edlund

To order this book, send $20 plus $3 shipping and handling to the publisher (Minnesota residents, please add an additional $1.30 for Minnesota sales tax):

Germanic Genealogy Society
P.O. Box 16312
St. Paul Minn. 55116-0312

First Printing, October 1995

Library of Congress cataloging in publication data

Edlund, Thomas Kent.
       Die Ahnenstammkartei des Deutschen Volkes: an introduction and register / by Thomas Kent Edlund.
          p.   cm.
          ISBN 0-9644337-2-9
          1. Genealogy--Catalogs. 2. Deutsche Zentralstelle für Genealogie--Catalogs. 3. Die Ahnenstammkartei des Deutschen Volkes--Catalogs. 4. Germany--Genealogy--Catalogs. I. Zentralstelle für Personen- und Familiengeschichte. II. Title.

                     95-076668
                     CIP

Abstract

Register to microreproduction of *Die Ahnenstammkartei des Deutschen Volkes* (Ancestor Lineage Card-File of the German People) and associated *Ahnentafeln* (ancestor charts) now housed at the *Deutsche Zentralstelle für Genealogie* (German Center for Genealogy) in Leipzig. Text provides access to all card indices and family pedigrees.

CONTENTS

Acknowledgements

I am grateful to LeRoy E. Niemann for the assistance given me in 1992-1993. Mr. Niemann's tenacity and linguistic skill provided a significant contribution to the preliminary draft of this project. Similar appreciation is due Michael Broschinsky for his proofing and verification of the *Ahnentafeln* (ancestor charts) reconstruction. I am likewise indebted to Tab A. M. Thompson for his work with the introduction to this text, and to the Editorial Board of the Germanic Genealogy Society, which supervised the book's publication.

Preface

Die Ahnenstammkartei des deutschen Volkes (ASTAKA)[1] was established in the city of Dresden by Dr. Karl Förster. In English, The *Ahnenstammkartei* means "Ancestor Lineage Card-File of the German People." The primary goal of this organization was to assist participating genealogists in circulating and coordinating their research. From its inception, ASTAKA has adhered to the several guiding principles, including:

1) the entire line of any submission must be indexed on file cards

2) lines are to be recorded phonetically and organized first by surname and then by place of origin

3) all sources for the data should be accurately noted

4) conflicting data will be retained until clarified; the burden for clarification, however, is placed on the participating family

5) records must be submitted on standard forms.

By 1939 over 1.5 million people were included. A sample of the collection made in 1937 disclosed the following geographical distribution:

30% North German families
22% Middle German families
17% East German families
15% South German families
14% West German families.

---

[1] Originally known as the *Ahnenlistenaustausch* (ALA) (Ancestor List Exchange) , *Die Ahnenstammkartei des deutschen Volkes* had its beginning in Dresden 1921. Dr. Karl Förster, a lawyer and Land Court Director, established the organization as an extension of the *Zentralstelle für Personen- und Familiengeschichte* (Center for Personal and Family History). Located in Dresden until 1933, ASTAKA was moved to Berlin from 1933-1939, and was administered as a department of the *Reichssippenamt*. Following the German invasion of Poland, the ASTAKA records were relocated to Dresden, where they survived the ravages of war in a local cave. Kurt Wensch, a genealogist who reactivated submissions to the file in 1945, is credited with ASTAKA's survival. Numerous *Ahnentafeln*, nevertheless, were destroyed and are missing from this microreproduction.

A similar data sample taken in 1991 calculated Middle German pedigrees at 40%. At that time over 2.4 million index cards were on file, heavily focusing on the time period of 1659-1750.[2]

Maintained by the *Deutsche Zentralstelle für Genealogie* (German Center for Genealogy) since 1967, ASTAKA pedigree charts and index cards in this filming contain approximately 2,700,000 personal names, predominately of German families. All cards in the collection refer to ancestral family names and are filed phonetically in "*Adreßbuch*" (address book) fashion. This filing system attempts to collate variant spellings derived from a "root" name, e.g. Schulze, Schultz, Schultze, Scholz and Scholze all file as Schulz. Once a root form has been established for filing purposes, any name with the same sound values will be interfiled with it, even names which are not usually associated with each other. For example, Boch equals Pöge, and Feder equates to Vetter.

The rules for converting a name to a phonetic equivalent are:
a) When choosing between several forms of a name, select the clearest or shortest, e.g. Henig for Hennicke and Hennig.

b) Silent letters and diacritical marks are eliminated, e.g. Hahn becomes Han, Biene becomes Bin.

c) Double letters are counted as a single, e.g. Haan becomes Han, Habbel becomes Habel.

d) Unstressed final e is ignored; en, both within and at the end of a word, is eliminated. Bruchenhausen thus becomes Bruchaus.

e) The suffix -sen and the genitive -s are dropped.

f) The letter e replaces ae and ä.

g) Eu replaces aeu and äu.

---

[2]Genealogists wishing to research ASTAKA are encouraged to first trace their family lines back to c. 1800 by other sources.

h) Ei replaces ai and ay.

i) Low German oe becomes u.

j) Eu replaces oi

k) High German oe and ö becomes o.

l) U replaces ue and ü.

m) I replaces y.

n) B replaces p.

o) C replaces ck, k, g, gk, k, ch, and cz (not initial).

p) X replaces cs, chs, gs and ks.

q) D replaces dt and t.

r) Z replaces ds, ts, dz and tz.

s) F replaces bf and pf.

t) H is used only when pronounced (see b above).

u) I replaces j.

v) F replaces ph.

w) Sc replaces dsch, tsch, dzsch and tzsch.

x) Schm replaces the sm of Low German.

y) The Low German sl becomes scl.

z) F replaces v and w.

These rules are valid only for High German names. Low German names should be left in their dialectical form, e.g. Voss cannot become Fuchs, nor Piper Pfeifer. For a complete explanation of foreign and Low German names, see the *Vorwort* (preface) on film number 1799712, item 3.

SUMMARY TABLE

ä	filed as	e	dt	filed as	d	ph	filed as	f
ae	"	e	dz	"	z	q	"	q
äu	"	eu	dzsch	"	sc	sl (Nd.)	"	scl
aeu	"	eu	g	"	c	sm (Nd.)	"	schm
ai	"	ei	gk	"	c	t	"	d
ay	"	ei	gs	"	x	ts	"	z
bf	"	f	j	"	i	tz	"	z
ch	"	c	k	"	c	tzsch, tsch	"	sc
chs	"	x	ks	"	x	ü	"	u
ck	"	c	ö, oe	"	o	ue	"	u
cs	"	x	oe (Nd.)	"	u	v	"	f
cz	"	c	oi	"	eu	w	"	f
ds	"	z	p	"	b	y	"	i
dsch	"	sc	pf	"	f			

READING THE CARDS

The following symbols are used in the Ahnenstammkartei:

x	birth	o	engagement	⚔	death in battle
~	christening	∞	marriage	†	deaths
o-o	illegitimacy	o/o	divorce	□	burials

Additional occupational signs and text words are used in a self-evident way, e.g. Bg equals Bürger and Jotus equals lawyer (Juris consultus).
Church membership is recorded at the top right in abbreviated form, e.g. ev.-luth., ev.-ref., r.-kath., menn. The Jewish faith is designated by a darkened triangle standing on its point (▼).

Cards of the *Ahnenstammkartei* are written on both sides. If a longer lineage has more than one card, it is serialized with Roman numerals on the right edge. As a rule, two generations are entered on the front side, and three on the reverse.

Surnames are written on the upper left hand corner. Coded source references, usually a four digit number preceded by AL, appear on the right. These AL numbers refer to the *Ahnentafeln* (full pedigrees) and are sequentially listed in part II of this register. Source codes of stepancestors are preceded by a slash (/). Supplementary references are indicated by Arabic numerals (1, 2, 3, etc.) near the four digit *Ahnenlisten* (AL) code.

Every family tree begins with a female name, excepting illegitimate fathers, male stepancestors, and males submitting their own pedigrees. All given names appear directly under the surname and are underlined. The given name a person uses (*Rufnamen*) is underlined twice. Under the female name appears the relevant birth and death dates, both on the same line. Information on marriages and spouses is recorded after this line.

The **Introduction** to this volume consists of an English translation of the German *Vorwort* mentioned above. This document describes in detail how the ASTAKA records are arranged, and additionally provides instructions for submitting family history information. If the user of this register finds these instructions inadequate, I refer them to any of the numerous journal articles available in professional genealogical literature.[3]

This register is organized into two main sections. Part I includes the following indices:

1) *Die Ahnenstammkartei* [Surname cards]: provides family name, given name, occupation or title, date and place of birth, marriage and death, name of spouse, religious affiliation

2) *Einsenderkartei* [Submitter cards]

---

[3]One of the better examples is: Ferguson, Laraine K. and Larry O. Jensen, "*Die Ahnenstammkartei des deutschen Volkes*: Pedigree Collection from Leipzig, Germany," German Genealogical Digest, 9 no. 4 (Winter 1993): 110-124.

3) *Ahnenlisten-Nummernkartei* [Ancestor lists by submission number]

4) *Berühmtenkartei* [Celebrity/Nobility index]

5) *Ortskartei* [Locality index]: lists places based on *Meyers Orts- und Verkehrs-Lexikon des Deutschen Reiches*.

6) *Sachkartei* [Vocation and Subject index]

7) *Nummernkartei* [Data source code cards].

Part II is a sequential listing of AL (*Ahnentafeln*) numbers cross-referenced to their corresponding microfilm and item number.

As a final note, I warn the researcher that ASTAKA has evolved over a 70 year period. Despite claims to the contrary, rules of indexing and organization have not been consistently or rigorously applied. In most cases, a certain amount of creative and intuitive searching is required for a successful result. I am certain that genealogists and family historians are more than equal to this challenge.

Thomas K. Edlund
Associate Librarian of Slavic Bibliography
Family History Library

INTRODUCTION

The Organization of the Ahnenstammkartei

1)   Each card of the *Ahnenstammkartei* refers to an ancestral family. All cards are grouped phonetically. This phonetic arrangement attempts to bring together variant spellings of family names and makes identification as easy as possible. Similar surnames have been grouped in two ways:

a) various spellings of the same root name are collated under a standard form (Schultz for Schulze, Schulz, Scholz, Scholtze, etc.),

b) names that sound similar but in fact have unrelated origins are treated as the same (Bock = Poge; Feder = Vetter, etc.).

Rules "a" and "b" may be used concurrently.

2)   The principle rules for converting a family name to a phonetic equivalent are as follows:

a) for names that have multiple spellings, select the "purest" or shortest form (Schulz = Scholtze; Andreas = Andres and Andresen; Henig = Henning, Hennicke and Haemichen, etc.).

b)   eliminate silent letters or linguistic length marks (Thalheim becomes Talheim; Hahn becomes Han; Biene and Biehn become Bin).

c) treat double letters as single letters (Han for Haan; Ber for Bär and Baer; Habel for Habbel; Rider for Ridder: Graf for Graff).

d) Ignore unstressed e and en in both the middle and at the end of names (Brunn for Bruhne; Schoenberg for Schoenenberg; Bruchaus for Bruchenhausen). Stressed e is retained (Schultetus remains Schultetus). When en follows r, the syllable is contracted to rn (Dörenberg becomes Dörnberg, not Dörberg).

e) Drop the final syllable -sen and the genitive -s (Franks and Francksen become Frank).

f) The letter e replaces ae and ä (Ber instead of Baer and Bär).

g) The diphthong eu replaces äu and aeu (Beumer for Baumer).

h) The diphthong ei replaces ai and ay (Beier instead of Baier or Bayer).

i) For oe (pronounced "u" in Low German) use u (Blum for Bloem).

k) The sound eu is used to replace oi (Heustreu instead of Hoiestroi); however, use rule "2a" for Voigt or Voit, which becomes Vogt and is filed as Focd.

l) For oe (pronounced ö in High German), use o (Bom for Bohme and Boehm).

m) The letter u replaces ue and ü (Schumann for Schümann).

n) The letter i replaces y.

o) The letter b replaces p (Baul replaces Paulsen).

p) The letter c replaces ck, k, g, gk, ch and cz (when cz does not begin the name): e.g. Kluck becomes Cluc, Christ becomes Crist; Egel, Eggle and Eckel to Ecel; Korback to Corbac.

q) Substitute x for cs, chs, gs, and ks (when ks ends a syllable); e.g. Wachsmuth becomes Waxmud.

r) Substitute d for dt and t (Deufel for Toifel).

s) The letter z replaces ds and ts, except when in contradiction to "2e."

t) The letter z also replaces dz and tz, as in Dezner for Tetzner.

u) The letter f replaces bf and pf, as in Feifer for Pfeifer.

v) The aspiration h is only retained when pronounced (when h begins a syllable). For example, h is not pronounced in Gayhe and Blühermann. Following rule "2b," Gayhe becomes Cei, and Blühermann becomes Bluerman. In contrast, Imhof remains Imhof, and Helborn.

w) The letter j becomes i.

x) Ph becomes f (Filib replaces Phillip).

y) The letter q remains q.

z) Sc replaces dsch, tsch, dzsch and tzsch (Tzschöltzsch becomes Scolsc).

aa) Sm in Plattdeutsch becomes schm (Smalenbier to Schmalbier).

bb) Sl in Plattdeutsch becomes scl (Slentz to Sclentz).

cc) The letter f replaces v and w (Voigt becomes Focd).

3) Medieval name spellings must be changed to modern spellings before applying the preceding rules.

4) The application of these phonetic conversion rules cannot lead to the destruction of the syllables forming the basic name stem (Brettschneider cannot become Breschneider, but rather Bredscneider).

5) These rules are generally valid only for German names. They apply by extension to names of Latin and Greek derivation. They do not apply to names of non-Germanic origin. Such names are filed alphabetically, with double letters counting as single. An exception is made with the initial letters of the name, where the phonetic rules apply. Separately written prefixes are ignored when filing, e.g. le Blanc and de la Porte.

6) Low German names are left in their original form, since it is rarely possible to trace a Low German name to a High German one. For example, Voss does not become Fuchs, and Piper does not become Pfeifer. When in doubt, treat Low German names as if they are non-Germanic.

7) Latin, Greek and French translations of German names (most frequently scholarly names) are to be converted back to German (Bohemus becomes Bom; Crusius becomes Craus). Valid Latin, Greek and French names are not to be translated. For example, Agricola is not to become Bauer or Landmann. If translations are made, a "see reference" card must be included. For Latin names, drop the terminal endings -us, -ius, -aeus [-asus?]. The Lithuanian ending -us is to be retained. Nobility titles and designations of origin are ignored (von Angern becomes Ancer; Graf v. Bülow becomes Bulof; Müller v. Berneck becomes Müller/Muler).

8) The suffixes -er and -erer are retained.

9) In southern German names that have omitted an e, the e must be restored to return the name to its most commonly used form (Gefatter becomes Cefader; Gsell becomes Cesel; Gwinner becomes Cefiner).

10) If the application of the preceding rules creates difficulty in finding a name, a reference card should be attached.

Instructions for Creating the Ahnenstammkartei

Script   1) File cards, for reasons of space, are to be typewritten, when possible or hand printed in ink. The small letter u is to be printed with a hook to distinguish it from the letter n.

Symbols   2) The following symbols are used for vital events: births = x; baptisms = ~; deaths = †; fallen in action = ⚔ ; burials = ☐; engagements = o; marriages = ∞; divorces = o/o; common law marriages = o-o.

3) Additionally, occupational abbreviations and text words may be used in a self-evident way (Bg. = Bürger, Brgmst. = Bürgermeister, Mstr. = Meister, Jotus = juris consultus (Rechtsanwalt).

Religion   4) An abbreviation of religious affiliation is placed at the top of the card next to the surname, i.e. ev.-luth., ev.-ref, r.-kath., menn; the Jewish faith is designated by a darkened upside down triangle (▼). If there is a change in religion within a lineage, the new abbreviation should be noted by the individual's name.

Organ-
ization 5) Information will be written on both sides of the card. If lineages require multiple cards, those cards must be numbered in the top right corner with roman numerals (I, II, III, etc.).

6) The information described in items 1-5 is to be written so that supplementary material can be added later, either above or below the line. An example of this is date changes. Generally, each card will have two generations written on the front and three on the back.

7) The surname is entered at the top left side of the card. A primary source is written on the upper right side. Additional sources are placed to the left of the main source and are separated with commas. The second line likewise begins on the right side and is used for AL codes (written in pencil) referencing supplemental information in other lineages. When necessary a third line of references may be used.

8) Each card (of a family line) begins with a female. Exceptions: pedigrees of male submitters, common law fathers and male step-ancestry. The given name of an ancestor begins at the left; the surname of the spouse ends at the right. Additional marriages are indented from the left. On the line introducing the pedigree, write only the name. The space following a female given name remains blank, when that name begins a family line. Write the birth date under the first given name one centimeter from the left edge. Enter the death date on the same line if there is room.

9) If several siblings are identified from the same family, the given names are uniformly indented one centimeter from the left edge of the card.

V.

```
┌─────────────────────────────────────────────────┐
│ ┌───────────────────────────────────────────────┐ │
│ │  Berger, ev.-luth.                       6014   │ │
│ ├───────────────────────────────────────────────┤ │
│ │                                                 │ │
│ ├───────────────────────────────────────────────┤ │
│ │     Hildegard Beate                             │ │
│ │          x Dresden (St.A.J) 15.9.1936           │ │
│ │          ~ das. (Kreuzk.) 1.10.                 │ │
│ │     Karl Friedrich                              │ │
│ │          x Dresden (St.A. III) 2.4.1939         │ │
│ │          ~ das. (Annenk.) 25.4                  │ │
│ └───────────────────────────────────────────────┘ │
└─────────────────────────────────────────────────┘
```

R.

```
┌─────────────────────────────────────────────────┐
│ ┌───────────────────────────────────────────────┐ │
│ │                                                 │ │
│ │  Friedrich Karl, Kaufmann in Dresden            │ │
│ │  x Leipzig (St.A. II) 16.8.1910                 │ │
│ │  ∞ Leipzig (St.A. III) 1.11.1935 Mathilde Schmidt│ │
│ │                                                 │ │
│ │  Carl August, Tischlermstr. in Leipzig          │ │
│ │  x das. (Nicol.) 11.2.1874  + Meissen/Sa.3.4.1930│ │
│ │  ∞ das.        6.7.1904     Helene Müller        │ │
│ │                                                 │ │
│ └───────────────────────────────────────────────┘ │
└─────────────────────────────────────────────────┘
```

Given name 10) All given names are underlined; the given name by which a person is known is underlined twice.

Step-ancestors 11) Stepancestors are indicated by a vertical line before the AL number, e.g. |9801.

Sources 12) Source references are recorded as coded symbols (signature). For a pedigree chart a number is sufficient (i.e. without "AL"). Supplementary information is coded by a "n1," "n2," etc., and is written as superscript immediately following the AL number. The AL number and the supplementary data are connected by a plus sign (+). Multiple additions are separated by commas, e.g. $4359^{+n2,3,4}$. Additional sources are connected to the original by a bow either above or to the side of the numbers, e.g. $101\overset{\frown}{5,}650$; or $1015\underset{650}{\big)}$.

Capital letters (other than AL) that prefix numbers are part of an older filing system, and should be included, e.g. F 10, N 529.

13) Archive entries are preceded by the letter "A." These entries require a source citation, e.g. S. 29, Bd. III, A 2638.

14) Cards lacking a source citation must list the name and residence of the submitter together with the date of submission. This is recorded on the second line of the card (Br. 07.08.56).

15) A time period (year) must appear on each card. If the source does not include a date, the submitter may estimate the time period, e.g. married before 1851 (when the source lists a child's birth in 1851). If the date cannot be so determined, use other information.

Meier	2355
Anna Maria x ∞	Martin Kraus 1673 Pastor in Stalsund †

16) Calculated dates are to be written with pencil in brackets and inset. Space for the actual date is left blank for later use.

Locality Data

17) Every card will have locality information. As a rule, the *Ahnenlisten Ortsverzeichnis* should be sufficient to determine the location and/or *Kreis* designation; this is the ancestor list place directory. If this fails, consult an appropriate gazetteer. If no localities are listed on a pedigree, list the location of the spouse. If the place name is common, specify the probable area in pencil, e.g.

x Altendorf um 1630   wohl über Bad Schandau/Elbe

If a locality has changed name, it is the rule to use the current form and enclose the older form in parentheses e.g. Bautzen/Sa. (fr. Budissin). For communities incorporated from smaller independent villages, list the name of the village first and then the modern name, e.g. Elberfeld (j. zu Wuppertal); Deutsch-Wilmersdorf (j. zu Berlin). Exception : When the source lists Chemnitz/Sa., enter as Chemnitz/Sa. (j. Karl-Marx-Stadt).

For localities that were part of the German Empire [but are not in modern Germany], use the old German name followed by the modern name, e.g. Breslau (j. Wrocław); Karlsbad (j. Karlovy Vary).

Should the same locality be repeated in the same line, it may be recorded as "das." This abbreviation only refers to the locality immediately preceding it. If the place of death is missing from the vital information (birth, marriage, death), the marriage locality will be written out even if it is identical to the birth city. (Should the place of death be identified later, it may be different from the place of marriage [or birth]), for example:

x A-dorf   † ...   or x B-dorf   † das.
∞ A-dorf   ∞ das.

The *Kreis* was not the local level of administration in all areas of pre-1940 Germany. The following designations appear in older gazetteers:

Baden: Amtsbezirk; Bayern: Bezirksamt; Oldenburg: Amt; Sachsen: Amtshauptmannschaft; Württemberg: Oberamt

Use Kr. (*Kreis*) for all these levels of administration.

Source
Citations

18) If detailed biographical information concerning a person is available, include only the most recent or important. List details about where they studied, or with government officials and clergy, cite all places of service. The acquisition of citizenship is always recorded. When vital dates are absent, information such as the buying or selling of land can be substituted.

19) If the number of children is known, record it under the date of marriage, e.g.

∞ Berlin 12.5.1850   Karoline Müller
8 Kdr. (3 S., 5 T.)

20) If the place of birth and christening (or death and burial) are the same, record only the date of birth (or death). If the christening (or burial) occurred at a different locality, record the christening (or burial) date as well.

21) If a locality (e.g. Großstadt) has several churches or civil registration offices, record the name of the church or office number in parentheses after the place name. For example:

Hans Albert x Mehren 3.5., ∼ Meissen (St. Afra) 7.5.1850, † Blasewitz (j.z. Dresden)(St.A.IV) 1.10., □ Loschwitz (j.z. Dresden) 4.10.1890 ∞ Meissen (Frauenk.) 2.3.1873.

<u>Common Ancestors</u> 22) A source with "s.a.K." indicates that the ancestor has been associated with other lines in the *Ahnentafeln*. Use abbreviated or condensed information to clearly identify the individual. In the case of multiple marriages, record only the children born to the couple listed.

<u>Unknown Ancestry</u> 23) If it is unknown which marriage a child comes from, the names of all legal wives will be listed, one beneath the other. They are written one centimeter from the right edge, and not underlined. Under this, write *Ahnin unbekannt* [mother not known] in pencil. In these cases, record on line two the note "undetermined whether ancestor or stepancestor."

24) When a source notes a pedigree with "?" (undocumented), write *Ahnenzugehörigkeit unsicher* [relationship uncertain] in pencil on the second line of the card, even if the ancestry of his wife's is given.

<u>Illegit-imate Children</u> 25) In the case of illegitimate children whose natural father is known, the father's name is written with a line through it. The name of the mother with her partner (o-o) follows the name of the child.

Changes in Surname	26) For families whose surnames change from generation to generation (e.g. Ostfriesland, westfäl. Hofnamen [farm names]) the line will be filed in one complete sequence. With each generation the appropriate surname will be written following the given name. List all relevant surnames on the initial card. Make an additional card for each different surname. On each of these phonetically similar cards the surname will be underlined twice. This serves to accommodate different filings in the *Ahnenstammkartei* and indicates under which names they can be found.
Under-lining	27) In addition to given names (see no. 10 above) the surname of a woman marrying into a family is underlined. In the case of multiple marriages, only the name of the ancestor is underlined.
Colored Markings	28) [**The microfilming of the Ahnenstammkartei is in black & white. This section may be difficult or impossible to apply**]. Colored markings will be used to identify common ancestors in the following sequence: —, x, xx, xxx, o, oo, ooo. A red erasable colored pencil is used first, then yellow, brown, and violet.
"n.v." Persons	29) If the source lists a person who married into a line, but there is no separate file card for him, he is to be listed as "*n.v.*" [*nicht verkartet*, (not indexed)]. All known information about this individual must be recorded on the spouse's card. If this information is not already on the card, search the source documentation and extract the data. As a rule, people noted as "n.v." are 1) wives whose ancestry is unknown; 2) stepancestors with common occupations [farmers, millers, etc.] but not teachers, priests, government officials, military officers, executioners, or scholars; 3) people with migratory occupations, such as millers, shepherds, and tenant farmers.

Abbreviations and Signs

A . . . . *Archiv(e)* = library/archive
AL . . . . *Ahnen-Liste* = ancestor list
ALn . . . . *Ahnen-Listen* = ancestor lists
AR . . . . *Ahnen-Reihe* = pedigree

ASt . . . . *Ahnen-Stamm* = pedigree

b . . . . *bei* = by, near

Ber . . . . *Berichtigung(s)* = correction(s)

Br . . . . *Brief* = letter

D . . . . *Namen-Forscher* = name researcher

AG . . . . *Deutsche Adels-Genossenschaft*
= German Nobility Association

Dfr . . . . *Dauerfrage* = question of

eig . . . . *eigene* = own (adj.)

eigener. d. . . . . *eingereicht durch* = submitted by

Erg . . . . *Ergänzung* = supplement

Fam. Gesch . . . . *Familien-Geschichte* = family history

Fr . . . . *Frage* = question

Frbg . . . . *Fragebogen* = questionnaire

Geschl . . . . *Geschlecht* = gender

Hb . . . . *Handbücher(ei)* = reference books or library

Jh . . . . *Jahrhundert* = century

K . . . . *Kinderliste* = list of children (from a compilation of students in Berlin, 1935)

Ma . . . . *Mappe* = file/folder

M.-M . . . . *Mitglieder-Meldung (bezog sich auf Mitgliedsveränderungen im Verkehr zwischen Vereinskanzlei Dresden und Abt. Ahnenstamm-Kartei im Reichssippenamt Berlin* = communication of membership status between the Dresden Society and the *Reichssippenamt* in Berlin)

M.-No . . . . *Mitglieds-Nummer* = membership number

Mgl. No . . . . *Mitglieds-Nummer* = membership number

N . . . . *Nichtmitglied* = non-member

NL . . . . *Neu-Liste (in der Einsenderkartei auch gebraucht für: Nichtmitglieder-Liste; Nachtrags-Liste; Nachfahren-Liste)* new list (used in the submitter index also for: non-member lists; supplement lists; descendant lists)

NfL . . . . *Nachfahren-Liste* = descendant list(s)

NfT . . . . *Nachfahren-Tafel* = descendant chart(s)

Ntr . . . . *Nachtrag* = supplement

n¹ usw . . . . *Nachtrag ¹ usw.* = supplement [1] etc.

o. J . . . . *ohne Jahr* = without year

o. O. u. J . . . . *ohne Ort und Jahr* = without place and year

P . . . . *Signatur für zur Filterung eingereichten Ahnenlisten eines Psychiatrischen Instituts in München* = label for the filtering of the genealogies submitted from the Psychiatric Institute of Munich

R . . . . *Roland (-Liste, auch -Mitglied)* = member list of the Roland Society

RfS . . . . *Reichsverein für Sippenforschung* = Imperial Society for Genealogy

s . . . . *seit* = since

s. a . . . . *siehe auch* = see also

SA. a. . . . . *Sonderausgabe aus* = special printing of

Sd . . . . *Sonderdruck* = special printing

SfR . . . . *Sachverständiger für Rasseforschung (Vorgänger des Reichssippenamtes)* Specialist in Ethnology (predecessor of the *Reichssippenamts*)

SL . . . . *Stamm-Liste* = pedigree

SR . . . . *Stamm-Reihe* = ancestral line

ST . . . . *Stamm-Tafel* = genealogical table

StB . . . . *Stamm-Baum* = pedigree chart

SV . . . . *Stamm-Vater* = progenitor (earliest known ancestor)

TlL . . . . *Teil-Liste* = partial list

TlNL . . . . *Teil-Neu-Liste* = partial new list

Translated by Thom. Edlund and Tab A. M. Thompson

REGISTER

REGISTER

Part I
Surname Index

```
Arnsdörfer - Arnheim, -hem ----------------------------- 1797811
Arn(en)old
      manuscripts
Arn(en)old
      by place: Annaberg - Lützen


Arn(en)old -------------------------------------------- 1797812
      by place: Marburg - Zwönitz, Neider-
Assmann, Ast-
      manuscripts
Assmann, Ast-
      by place: Ahlbeck - Stolzenburg


Assmeier - Aurea -------------------------------------- 1797813


Aures - Pappschin ------------------------------------- 1797814
Pabst, Papst, Bapst, etc.
      manuscripts
Pabst, Papst, Bapst, etc.
      by place: A - Büttelstedt


Pabst, Pabst, Bapst, etc. ----------------------------- 1797815
      by place: Büttelstedt - Zittau
v. Papstein - Pagel


Baccalarius - Pagenkopf ------------------------------- 1797816
Backofen
      manuscripts: Altefähr - Winter, Ober-


Backofen ---------------------------------------------- 1797817
      manuscripts: Weistenthin - Zurich
Backofen
      by place
Backenkohler - Bailly
Pahl
      manuscripts: Aalen - Eldena


Pahl -------------------------------------------------- 1797818
      manuscripts: Emden - Zopfenbeck
Pahl
      by place
Balack - Baller


Bahlert - Bantlin ------------------------------------- 1797819


v. Bandelin - Bargfrede ------------------------------- 1797820


Barckhahnen - v. Partein ------------------------------ 1797781
Bart(h)els, Bertel, Bart(h)old, Bert(hold)
      manuscripts: Aberzhausen - Iderhausen
```

```
Bart(h)els, etc.  ------------------------------------------- 1797782
      manuscripts: Edelsbüttel - Zweinert
Bart(h)els, etc.
      by place: Adelebsen - Penig


Bart(h)el, etc.  -------------------------------------------- 1797783
      by place: Preßnitz - Züllichau
Bartelmann - Baron


Barons - Basedow  ------------------------------------------ 1797784


Basedow  (cont.) - Baudouin  ------------------------------- 1797785
Bauer
      manuscripts: Aach - Wain/Kr. Biberach


Bauer  ----------------------------------------------------- 1797786
      manuscripts: Walbendorf - Zwönitz
Bauer
      by place
Bauerdiek - Bauhofer
Paul, Paulsen, Pauli, Paulus
      manuscripts: Aachen - Muhlstedt


Paul, Paulsen, Pauli, Paulus  ------------------------------ 1797787
      manuscripts: Mühlheim - Zwichau
Paul, Paulsen, Pauli, Paulus
      by place
Pauland - Paulun(owna)
Baum
      manuscripts: Althof - Wörstorf


Baum  ------------------------------------------------------ 1797788
      manuscripts: Woningen - Zielenzig
Baum
      by place
Baumacker - v. Baumburg
Baumgart
      manuscripts
Baumgart
      by place: Arnsdorf - Borken


Baumgart  -------------------------------------------------- 1797789
      by place: Godshorn - Worles
Baumgärtel - Bebel


Bäbel (cont.) - Päpke  ------------------------------------- 1797790
Beck
      manuscripts
Beck
      by place: Aichelberg - Pforzheim
```

```
Beck ------------------------------------------------------- 1797765
       by place: Raase (Freudental) - Zöblitz
Peccatel - Beken


Becker ----------------------------------------------------- 1797765
       manuscripts: Aachen - Neuheim


Becker ----------------------------------------------------- 1797766
       manuscripts: Neukirchen - Zwönitz
Becker
       by place: A. - Neukirchen


Becker ----------------------------------------------------- 1797767
       by place: Nidda - Zschorlau
Beckas - Pechlöffel
Beckmann
       manuscripts
Beckmann
       by place: Allendorf - Verden


Beckmann --------------------------------------------------- 1797768
       by place: Wehringhausen - Wolthausen
Beckmeier - v. Betaz
Beer(en), Behr, Bär
       manuscripts
Beer(en), Behr, Bär
       by place: Aschack - Gera


Beer(en), Behr, Bär ---------------------------------------- 1797769
       by place: Guben - Zittau
Perachon - Berbrok
Berg(e)
       manuscripts
Berg(e)
       without place


Berg(e) ---------------------------------------------------- 1797770
       without place (cont.)
Berg(e)
       by place: Altentreptow - Wesel
v. Berga - Berchend
Berger(s)
       manuscripts
Berger(s)
       by place: Andersdorf/Mähren - Dresden


Berger(s) -------------------------------------------------- 1797771
       by place: Dresden (cont.) - Zuftlich
Bergersdorfer - Berkling
Berg(e)mann
       manuscripts
Berg(e)mann
       by place: Andreasberg - Cochstedt
```

6

```
Berg(e)mann ------------------------------------------------- 1797772
        by place: Cochstedt - Zossen
Berkemeier - Perrin
Bering
        manuscripts: Alberg - Tidemannsholm


Bering ------------------------------------------------------ 1797773
        manuscripts: Trendelburg - Zbytzewice
Bering
        by place: Birkenheyde - Saalfeld
Bernd(t), Behrend(s), Bernhard
        manuscripts: Berlin - Jahnsdorf


Bernd, etc. ------------------------------------------------- 1797774
        manuscripts: Janswitz - Zwönitz, Nieder
Bernd, etc.
        by place: Altdorf - Leimbach


Bernd, etc. ------------------------------------------------- 1797801
        by place: Ladersleben - Züllichau
Bärschmidt - Pierson


Pierson - Betts --------------------------------------------- 1797802
Beu, Boy(en), Boje(n)
        manuscripts: Almdorf - Mühlhausen


Beu, etc. --------------------------------------------------- 1797803
        manuscripts: Münder - Klöster Zinna
Beu, etc.
        by place
Boysen - Peist


Beust (cont.) - Petznick ------------------------------------ 1797804
Pezold
        manuscripts
Pezold
        by place: Altenburg - Marienburg


Pezold ------------------------------------------------------ 1797805
        by place: Meerane - Zabelsdorf/Brdg.
Bötzel - Bitterberg


Biderberg (cont.) - Pielenz -------------------------------- 1797806
Bie(h)ler, Biller(t), Büler
        manuscripts: Aalen - Wustenrot


Bie(h)ler, etc. -------------------------------------------- 1797807
        manuscripts: Wunsiedel - Zwirtzschen
Bie(h)lrt, etc.
        by place
Pillera - Bind
```

```
Bind  (cont.) - Bierer ----------------------------------- 1797808


Bührer - Bischoping ------------------------------------ 1797809
Bischoff
      manuscripts: Aachen - Gangelt


Bischoff ----------------------------------------------- 1797810
      manuscripts: Gartz - Zwenkau
Bischoff
      by place
Bischoffberger - Plagmann


Plagmann  (cont.) - Bedenk ------------------------------ 1797791
Peter(s), Petersen, Petri, etc.
      manuscripts: Aachen - Etzdorf


Peter(s), etc. ----------------------------------------- 1797792
      manuscripts: Etzdorf - Volpriehausen
Peter(s), etc.
      by place: Allendorf - Herborn


Peter(s), etc. ----------------------------------------- 1797793
      by place: (Forts) Hildesheim - Zwickau
Petersberger - Petrischer


Petro - Beydemüller ------------------------------------ 1797794
Bayer
      manuscripts


Bayer -------------------------------------------------- 1797795
      by place
Beyerbach - Peyinkuck
Beil(e), Beyl(1), Beyel, Pleil(1), Beule
      manuscripts, Spezialliste u. Adel


Bayer -------------------------------------------------- 1797796
      Adel (cont.)
Bayer
      by place
Beiler(t) -ai, - Pelhamer


Belhase - Bennau --------------------------------------- 1797797
Ben(c)ke, Ben(n)cke, Pen(c)ke
      manuscripts
Ben(c)ke, etc.
      by place: Aenze - Stadthagen


Ben(c)ke, etc. ----------------------------------------- 1797798
      by place: Stolp - Würselen
Benekamp - Bennighoff
```

```
Bennighoven - Blanbois ----------------------------------- 1797799
Blan(c)ke, Plan(c)k
      manuscripts
Blan(c)ke, etc.
      by place: Altona - Liebenrode


Blan(c)ke, etc. ----------------------------------------- 1797800
      by place: Penzlin - Zwickau
Blanchau - Blaich


Bleick(en) - Blöchner ----------------------------------- 1797775


Blöckner (cont.) - Pluis -------------------------------- 1797776
Blume(n), Blome
      manuscripts
Blume(n), Blome
      by place: Barmstadt - Steinkirchen


Blume(n), Blome ----------------------------------------- 1797777
      by place: Tangermünde - Zeppernick
Plümacher - Poppelmann


Poppelmann (cont.) - Bobsnzan --------------------------- 1797778
Bock, Boge(n), Pogge, Poch
      manuscripts
Bock, etc.
      by place: Basel - Oldendorf


Bock, etc. ---------------------------------------------- 1797779
      by place: Ostrau - Zimmeritz
Pocabis - Bogun


Bochur - v. Bodeghenz ----------------------------------- 1797780
Böttcher, Bottger, Boetticher
      manuscripts: Aachen - Lillienthal


Böttcher, etc. ------------------------------------------ 1798490
      manuscripts: Luhan b. Gera - Zwönitz
Böttcher, etc.
      by place
Pottgießer - v. Poderwils


v. Poderwils (cont.) - Bojunga ------------------------- 1798491
Bolle, Bohl, Polle, Pohl
      manuscripts


Bolle, etc. -------------------------------------------- 1798492
      by place
Pola - Polkow
Bolte, Bolten, Boldt
      manuscripts
```

```
Bolte, etc.  ---------------------------------------------- 1798492
      by place
Bolta - Bohlmacher ---------------------------------------- 1798493
Bohlmann, Bollmann, Pohlmann
      manuscripts
Bohlmann, etc.
      by place: Alfeld - Giebringhausen


Bohlmann, etc.  ------------------------------------------- 1798494
      by place: Halberstadt - Zeuleroda
Boehm, Boehme
      manuscripts: Aachen - Salzwedel


Boehm, etc.  --------------------------------------------- 1798495
      manuscripts: Sandersleben - Zwönitz
Backmann - Boomgaerd


Bohmgarn - Pomzel ---------------------------------------- 1798496
Bohn, Bohnen, Bonn (Bonse, Bons)
      manuscripts
Bohn, etc.
      by place: Aachen - Lübeck


Bohn, etc.  --------------------------------------------- 1798497
      by place: Neukirchen - Zeitz
Bohne - Bonnet


Bonnet  (cont.) - Borth --------------------------------- 1798498


Bortz - Börner ------------------------------------------ 1798499


Pirner - Pospisil --------------------------------------- 1798500
Bosch, Poetsch
      Schrifum: Aachen - Mehrstetten


Bosch, etc.  -------------------------------------------- 1798501
      manuscripts: Mehssow - Zwochau
Bosch, etc.
      by place
v. Potschach - Boseque
Poser, Posern, Bossert
      manuscripts: Abertham - Schwarzhausen


Poser, etc.  -------------------------------------------- 1798502
      manuscripts: Sessen - Zullichau
Poser, etc.
      by place
Poserien - Brackenhoff
```

Bracklau - Branger --------------------------------- 1798503
Brandt, Brandes, Brandis
      manuscripts
Brandt, etc.
      by place: Aachen - Barleben

Brandt, etc. --------------------------------------- 1798504
      by place: Barlenleben - Zulow
Brandauer - Prasse

Brasch - v. Praumheim ------------------------------ 1798505
Braun(en), Praun, Brauhn(s)
      manuscripts: Aach - Ruwer Kr. Trier

Braun(en), etc. ------------------------------------ 1798506
      manuscripts: Saalfeld - Weissenburg
Braun(en), etc.
      by place: Aachen - Reutlingen

Braun(en), etc. ------------------------------------ 1798507
   by place: Reutlingen - Zürich
Braunau(er) - Bretner

Bredner - Preller ---------------------------------- 1798508

v. Prellwitz - Brenneisen -------------------------- 1798509

Brennhausen - Breul -------------------------------- 1798440

Breul - Preussensin -------------------------------- 1798441
Preusser, Preisser
   manuscripts
Preusser, Preisser
   Literature

Preusser, Preisser --------------------------------- 1798442
   Literature (cont.)
Preuswerck - Brisch(ke), Brusch

Brisch(ke), Brusch (cont.) - Brogler -------------- 1798443

Bröcklin - Brosch, Brösicke, Brosio, Brozio -------- 1798444

Brosch, Brösicke, Brosio, Brozio (forts.) --------- 1798445
Brückmann
   manuscripts
Brückmann
   by place: Apelern - Mölln

Brückmann --- 1798446
    by place: Osnabrück - Unna
Bruckmeier, Brockmeir - Brum(m)er

Brumer (cont.) - Bube --- 1798447

Bube (cont.) - Buchholder --------------------------------------- 1798448

Buchholz -- 1798449
    manuscripts
Buchholz
    by place
Buchhorn - v. Buggnem
Buchner, Buckner, Bucher
    manuscripts
Buchner, etc.
    by place: Augsbug - Grafentonna

Buchner, etc. --- 1798430
    by place: Jena - Zeppenfeld
Buchnowski - Butenandt
Büttner, Bittner, Böttner
    Scriftum: Abtsbessingen - Belmsdorf

Büttner, etc. --- 1798431
    manuscripts: Belzig, Kr. Zauch - Elsterberg
Büttner, etc.
    by place
Buttny - Buitz
Bull, Buhel, Puhl, Püll, Puls
    manuscripts: Aachen - Flintbeck

Bull, etc. -- 1798432
    manuscripts: Forst,NL - Trebs
Bull, etc.
    by place
Buland - Pumdsack

Bundschön - Burkamp -- 1798433
Burghard, Burkhart, Borghard, Burchard, Burgert
    manuscripts: Agra Lugano - Speckfeld

Burghard, etc. --- 1798434
    manuscripts: Speyer - Zwittau
Burghard
    by place
Burkas - Bürgel(t)
Burger
    manuscripts: Adorf - Bonn

Bürger --- 1798435
    manuscripts: Bopfingen - Zwickau
    by place

```
Burgertz- Puhrlich ---------------------------------------------- 1798435
Buhrmann, Bürmann, Bohrmann
      manuscripts
      by place: Eilenstedt - Celle


Buhrmann, etc. -------------------------------------------------- 1798436
      manuscripts: Köln - Witten
Burme(i)ster - Burzlaff
Busse
      manuscripts


Busse ----------------------------------------------------------- 1798437
      by place
Pusack - Bußgahn
Busch, Büsch(e), Pusch, Putsch
      manuscripts


Busch, etc. ----------------------------------------------------- 1798438
      by place
Buschak - Buschler
Buschmann
      manuscripts
Buschmann
      by place: A. - Mildenau


Buschmann ------------------------------------------------------- 1798439
      by place: Sachsenhagen - Zwickau
Buschmeyer - Dacho


Daggob - Tallowitz ---------------------------------------------- 1798667
Damm
      manuscripts: Aachen - Taubenheim


Damm ------------------------------------------------------------ 1798668
      manuscripts: Tellschütz - Zweimen
Damm
      by place
Dammann - Tantau


Tandl - Dau(e)l ------------------------------------------------- 1798669
Daume
      manuscripts: Altenlotheim - Falkenhorst


Daume ----------------------------------------------------------- 1798670
      manuscripts: Fraustadt - Zwickau
Daume
      by place
Daumann - Dechent
Decker
      manuscripts
Decker
      by place: Altenburg - Rainrod
```

Decker -- 1798647
        by place: Reutlingen - Züllichau
v. Tegerfeld - Taiglieber
Deichmann
        manuscripts: Adolzfurt - Aurauff

Deichmann --- 1798648
        manuscripts: Arendsee - Zwickau
Deichmann
        by place
Teichmeyer - Delong

Delömen - Denham -- 1798649

Denhard - Deublinger -- 1798650
Teubner
        manuscripts

Teubner --- 1798651
        by place
Teutenbuhl - Tippann

Tiebe - Thieden --- 1798652

Tidde - v. Ditmansdorf -------------------------------------- 1798653
Ditmar, Dittmer, Detmar
        manuscripts: Aachen - Suhl

Dietmar, etc. --- 1798654
        manuscripts: Sulzbach - Zwickau
Dietmar, etc.
        by place
Dietmarkhausen - Titot
Dietrich
        manuscripts
Dietrich
        by place: Adelsdorf - Gustrow

Dietrich -- 1798655
        by place: Halberstadt - Ziesel
Didszun - Tyhoff u. Thiehove
Thiel, Diehl
        manuscripts: Aachen - Rambin

Thiele, etc. -- 1798656
        manuscripts: Ramstadt - Zwingenberg
Thiele, etc.
        by place
Dillan - Tilem

```
Dieler - Tilzig u. Tilzog ------------------------------- 1798657
Thiem
      manuscripts
Thiem
      by place: Amsterdam - Riga


Thiem ---------------------------------------------------- 1798658
      by place: Salzgitter - Zwickau
Tiemann - Thierfelder
Dirk, Dirik, Tierchen
      manuscripts
Dirk, etc.
      by place: Bloxdorf - Bremen


Dirk, etc. ---------------------------------------------- 1798659
      by place: Danzig - Wörden
Diergart - Dixon
Tietz, Titius
      manuscripts: Aachen - Gründ (Dresden)


Tietz, etc. --------------------------------------------- 1798660
      manuscripts: Gückelsberg - Zwickau
Titz, u. a
      by place
Dietzau - Döbel


Dobl - Dopfeld ------------------------------------------ 1798661
Töpfer
      manuscripts: Achelstadt - Wehrau (Bunzlau)


Töpfer -------------------------------------------------- 1798662
      manuscripts: Weimar - Zirkau
Töpfer
      by place
Dowey - Domanetzki
Thomas, Thomae, Thomsen
      manuscripts: Aachen - Heineberg


Thomas, etc. -------------------------------------------- 1798663
      manuscripts: Helbigsdorf - Zweinig
Thomas, etc.
      by place
Damaschke - Tomzig
Ton, Thön
      manuscripts


Ton, etc. ----------------------------------------------- 1798664
      by place
v. Dohna - Dorper


Dorper (cont.) - Dorlath -------------------------------- 1798665
```

```
Dorland - Dozler (-u-) ----------------------------------- 1798666


Dotzenrod - Travella ------------------------------------- 1798868
Treger
        manuscripts
Treger
        by place: Annaberg - Dorfchemnitz


Treger --------------------------------------------------- 1798869
        by place: Greifenberg - Zschorlau
Dregler - Drescher


Trescher (cont.) - Triebel ------------------------------- 1798870


Triebel (cont.) - Droschütz ------------------------------ 1798871
Drost
        manuscripts: Aachen - Krefeld


Drost ---------------------------------------------------- 1798872
        manuscripts: Crispenhofen - Zittau
Drost
        by place
Trostorf - Dücker


Duker (cont.) - Dünckel ---------------------------------- 1798873


Tunkel (cont.) - Durbrecht ------------------------------- 1798874
Türk
        manuscripts: Ansbach - Wasungen


Türk ----------------------------------------------------- 1798875
        manuscripts: Weiden - Zerbst
Türk
        by place
v. Dürckheim - Ept
Ebel
        manuscripts
Eble
        by place


Eppelsheim - Ebendig ------------------------------------- 1798876
Ebert, Ewert, Eberhardt, Ebhard
        manuscripts
Ebert, etc.
        by place: Altenburg - Hohenstein


Ebert, etc. ---------------------------------------------- 1798877
        by place: Isny - Zwickau
v. Eberhorst - Ebser
Eck
        manuscripts
```

```
Eck ----------------------------------------------------- 1798877
     by place: Augsburg - Averfleth


Eck ----------------------------------------------------- 1798838
     by place: Dieburg - Weissenburg
Eckart, Eckhart, Eger
     manuscripts
Eckart, etc.
     by place: Altendorf - Gera


Eckart, etc. -------------------------------------------- 1798839
     by place: Gotha - Wurzen
Echternach - Egenolf
Eckold
     manuscripts


Eckold -------------------------------------------------- 1798840
     by place
Eckel - Eig(en)


Eicke(n)  (cont.) - Eickenroth --------------------------- 1798841


v. Eickenscheidt - Eisenlower --------------------------- 1798842


Eisenlohr  (cont.) - Elentzer ---------------------------- 1798843
Ehler, Oehler
     manuscripts
Ehler, etc.
     by place: Bendhof - Vienna


Ehler, etc. --------------------------------------------- 1798844
     by place: Wittstock - Zehna
v. Ellerbach - v. Emershofen
Emmerich
     manuscripts
Emmerich
     by place: Allendorf - Herold


Emmerich ------------------------------------------------ 1798845
     by place: Kusel - Venusberg
Emmerlein, -le, -lin, Engelbert
     manuscripts: Aachen - Paris/Fr.


Emmerlein, etc. ----------------------------------------- 1798846
     manuscripts: Pillau - Zwickau
Emmerlein, etc.
     by place
Engelbrunn(er), -bronn(er) - Engerwin
```

```
Engerkaus - Erasmus ------------------------------------------- 1798847
Erb, Erbs
        manuscripts
Erb, etc.
        by place: Altenroda - Friesenheim


Erb, etc.  ------------------------------------------- 1798858
        by place: Hermannseifen - Utendorf
v. Erbach - v. Erffortshausen
Erhard
        manuscripts
Erhard
        by place: Augsburg - Prettin


Erhard ------------------------------------------- 1798859
        by place: Schmalkalden - Weisslensburg
Ehrenhaus - Ernotte
Ernst
        manuscripts: Aachen - Groß Nossen


Ernst ------------------------------------------- 1798860
        manuscripts: Nottmark - Zwickau
Ernst
        by place
Ernstberger - Ekstedt


Estel - Wabst ------------------------------------------- 1798861
Wag
        manuscripts
Wag
        by place: A. - Northeim


Wag ------------------------------------------- 1798862
        by place: Forts.
Waga - Wagenknecht
Wagner
        manuscripts: Aachen - Mittlau


Wagner ------------------------------------------- 1798863
        manuscripts: Mittweida - Zwingenberg
Wagner
        by place: Aidlingen - Langenberg


Wagner ------------------------------------------- 1798864
        by place: Laufenfelden - Zwickau
Wagnitz - Waiuren
Wahl, Pfahl
        manuscripts: Aachen - Köln


Wahl ------------------------------------------- 1798865
        manuscripts: Köndringen - Wethen
Wahl
        by place
Walsen - Falkenhagen
```

```
v. Falkenhayn - Valthenius ----------------------------- 1798866
Walter
        manuscripts
Walter
        by place: Alsenborn - Arnstadt


Walter ------------------------------------------------- 1798867
        by place: Benneckenstein - Zwickau
Falterbaum - v. Waldner


v. Waldow - Fans(e) ------------------------------------ 1798848


Wansarts - Wasserfall ---------------------------------- 1798849


v. Wasserfass - Webel ---------------------------------- 1798850
Weber, Wever
        manuscripts: Ablass - Diedesheim


Weber, etc. -------------------------------------------- 1798851
        manuscripts: Dielbach - Zwönitz, Nieder-
Weber, etc.
        by place: Alsfeld - Fresdorf


Weber, etc. -------------------------------------------- 1798852
        by place: Freyenröthenbach - Zwönitz
Wehberg - v. Vechelde


Wegenka - Wedekin -------------------------------------- 1798853


Wedeking - Wetemoller ---------------------------------- 1798854


Vetmos - Feichtner ------------------------------------- 1798855
Weigel, Weigold
        manuscripts
Weigel, etc.
        by place: Affalter, Ober - Scheibenberg


Weigel, etc. ------------------------------------------- 1798856
        by place: Schönheide - Wildenau
Veigelheuser - v. Weyer


v. Weyer  (cont.) - Veilinger -------------------------- 1798857
Feil
        manuscripts
Feil
        by place: Alfeld - Güsten
```

```
Feil --------------------------------------------------------- 1798828
        by place: Lustnau - Weilmünster
Fehlan - Wejerowitz
Weiss(en), -see
        manuscripts: Aachen - Friedenau


Weiss, u. a --------------------------------------------------- 1798829
        manuscripts: Friedland (Czechoslovakia) - Zwoschwitz
Weiss, etc.
        by place: Adorf - Klaffenbach


Weiss, etc. --------------------------------------------------- 1798830
        by place: Koburg - Zwickau
Weisand - Weishaus


Weisheit - Wenzlaff ------------------------------------------- 1798831
Felger, Folger, Felcker
        manuscripts
Felger, etc.
        by place: Aken - Ilmenau


Felger, etc. -------------------------------------------------- 1798832
        by place: Kossendorf - Wipfra
Volguardtsen - Welensky
Feller, Foller, Wöhler
        manuscripts
Feller, etc.
        by place: Anderlingen - Bargstedt


Feller, etc. -------------------------------------------------- 1798833
        by place: Beeck - Alt-Zschillen
Wellerhaus - Vennebriegge
Wenk
        manuscripts


Wenk ---------------------------------------------------------- 1798834
        by place
Fenckel - Venendy
Wehner, Wöhner
        manuscripts
Wehner, etc.
        by place: Bautzen - Bischofswerda


Wehner, etc. -------------------------------------------------- 1798835
        by place: Hirselberg - Zegenhain
Wennehold - Fenzahn
Wehr
        manuscripts


Wehr ---------------------------------------------------------- 1798836
        by place
Ferrari - Verhey
```

```
Verheiden - Ferndran ------------------------------------- 1798837
Werner
        manuscripts: Aberode - Kaufungen


Werner ------------------------------------------------- 1798818
        manuscripts: Relle - Zwoschau
Werner
        by place: Adelsheim - Sommerfeld


Werner ------------------------------------------------- 1798819
        by place: Sontra - Zschoken
v. Vernezobre - v. Westerstetten
Westfal
        manuscripts
Westfal
        by place: Anklam - Lenfeld


Wersfal ------------------------------------------------ 1798820
        by place: Kankelfilz - Wedderstadt
Westfeld - Wetzer
Westzel
        manuscripts: Aachen - Heiligenrode


Wetzel ------------------------------------------------- 1798821
        manuscripts: Hofheim b. Worms - Zwönitz
Fetzer - Wiebusch
Fick
        manuscripts: Aarau - Landau


Fick --------------------------------------------------- 1798822
        manuscripts: Langenhausbergen -
        Zwischenahn
Wigandt - Fickelscherer


Fickelscherer  (cont.) - Wiczos ----------------------- 1798823
Wiede, Witte
        manuscripts: Aachen - Köthen


Wide, etc. --------------------------------------------- 1798824
        manuscripts: Kolberg - Zwickau
Wide
        by place
v. Vida - Witthar


Witthard - Wittke, Wittka u. Vitka --------------------- 1798825


Wittlich - Viehofer ------------------------------------ 1798826
Will
        manuscripts: Adelhofen - Arnheim
```

```
Will ------------------------------------------------------- 1798827
      manuscripts: Asbach - Zwickau
Wil
      by place
v. Vile - Wilburger
Wilke
      manuscripts: Aarhuus - Reval


Wilke ------------------------------------------------------ 1798739
      manuscripts: Ribnitz - Zwickau
Wilke
      by place
v. Wilchau - Philgus
Wild
      manuscripts
Wild
      by place: Auerbach i. V. - Leinfelden


Wild ------------------------------------------------------- 1798740
      by place: Melchingen - Zschorlau
Wildenthaler - Wilhely
Wilhelm
      manuscripts
Wilhelm
      by place: Amsterdam - Schmalkalden


Wilhelm ---------------------------------------------------- 1798741
      by place: Schwieberdingen - Wesel
Wilms - Wienprecht
Fink, Wink, Wienecke
      manuscripts: Aachen - Bremen


Fink ------------------------------------------------------- 1798742
      manuscripts: Breslau - Zusamaltheim
Fink
      by place
Fingado - Winkelmann


Winkelmann - Winkelhaus ------------------------------------ 1798743
Winkler
      manuscripts
Winkler
      by place: Altenburg - Viernheim


Winkler ---------------------------------------------------- 1798744
      by place: Wernsdorf - Zwickau
Finkmann - Winterstein


Windwege - Vircus ------------------------------------------ 1798745
Wirt
      manuscripts
Wirt
      by place: Borna b. Leipzig - Venrath
```

```
Wirth --------------------------------------------------- 1798746
      by place: Wartha - Zier
Vierthaler - Wiskemper
Fischer, Wisser
      manuscripts: Aachen -


Fischer, etc. ------------------------------------------- 1798747
      manuscripts: Aarau - Ulbersdorf (Switzerland)


Fischer, etc. ------------------------------------------- 1799896
      manuscripts: Ulm - Zwota, Zwickau
Fischer, etc.
      by place: Aerzen - Lanensalza


Fischer, etc. ------------------------------------------- 1799897
      by place: Lang-Göns - Zwönitz
Fischwasser - Pfisterer


Pfisterer  (cont.) - Flatz ------------------------------ 1799898


Flatz  (cont.) - Flender -------------------------------- 1799899


Flentge - Wobig ----------------------------------------- 1799900


Fobro - Fockenberg -------------------------------------- 1799901
Vogt, Voigts
      manuscripts: Aalen - Fleissa


Vogt, etc. ---------------------------------------------- 1799902
      manuscripts: Theissen - Zwolle (Netherlands)
Vogt, etc.
      by place
Vogtsberg - Vogding


Voightländer - Fögtner ---------------------------------- 1799903
Vogel
      manuscripts
Vogel
      by place: Aidlingen - Riesa


Vogel --------------------------------------------------- 1799904
      by place: Rodewisch - Zwickau
Vogelabacher - Wolk


Volck  (cont.) - Wohlleb -------------------------------- 1799905


Wollaib - Fohloi ---------------------------------------- 1799886
Wolf, Wulf
      manuscripts: Aachen - Wedderslaeben
```

```
Wolf, etc.  --------------------------------------------------- 1799887
        manuscripts: Weddingen - Zwolle
Wolf, etc.
        by place: Aachen - Nassau


Wolf, etc.  --------------------------------------------------- 1799888
        by place: Nassenhelde - Zwirtzschen
Wolfangel - Wolfhagen


Wolfhagen  (cont.) - Wolzendorf ------------------------- 1799889


Foltzer - Förstel ------------------------------------------- 1799890


Foerster - Werz --------------------------------------------- 1799891
Voss
        manuscripts: Aachen - Hüttenwohld


Voss  --------------------------------------------------------- 1799892
        manuscripts: Huisberden - Zwickau
Vossberg - Framolt
Frank
        manuscripts: Aachen - Pieverstorf


Frank  -------------------------------------------------------- 1799893
        manuscripts: Pirkensee - Zwota
Frankenbach - Fransoiser
Franz
        manuscripts: Aachen - Katz bei Danzig


Franz  -------------------------------------------------------- 1799894
        manuscripts: Kaufbach - Zwönitz
Franz
        by place
Franzenball - Freckenhorst
Frey
        manuscripts: Aarau (Switzerland) - Grabben


Frey  --------------------------------------------------------- 1799895
        manuscripts: Greuzach - Zwillikon (Switzerland)
Frey
        by place
Freyalthofer - Frenger


Pfränger - Friaul ------------------------------------------- 1799876
Frib(el), Froben, Fröbel, Fröbin, Freuel
        manuscripts:
Frib(el), etc.
        by place: Altendorf - Struth
```

```
Frib(el), etc.  --------------------------------------------- 1799877
        by place: Tonndorf bei Weimar - Zechau
Friche - Friedenreich
Friedrich, Friederich
        manuscripts: Aga - Ottendorf


Friedrich, etc.  -------------------------------------------- 1799878
        manuscripts: Olterwisch - Zwönitz
Friedrich, etc.
        by place
Friederaum - Friericks
Friese
        manuscripts: Aachen - Barssen


Friese  ----------------------------------------------------- 1799879
        manuscripts: Barth - Zwischenahn
Friese
        by place
v. Wriesberg - Friesslich
Fritsche
        manuscripts: Adelberg - Weissenfels


Fritsche  --------------------------------------------------- 1799880
        manuscripts: Weissensee - Zwönitz
Fritsche
        by place
Frischauer - Wrixon
Fritz
        manuscripts
Fritz
        by place: Arnswalde - Werben


Fritz  ------------------------------------------------------ 1799881
        by place: Wetzlar
Frittzel - Fübich


Wübbele - Wünaker  ------------------------------------------ 1799881
Funk(e)
        manuscripts
Funk(e)
        by place: Altenberg - Crumstadt


Funk(e)  ---------------------------------------------------- 1799883
        by place: Leipzig - Zwickau
Funckelte - v. Wummerode
Wünsch(mann)
        manuscripts
Wünsch(mann)
        by place: Annaberg - Thorn


Wünsch(mann)  ----------------------------------------------- 1799884
        by place: Uhlbach - Zittau
Wünschenmeier - Würtzner
```

```
Fues - v. Vusum ------------------------------------------- 1799885
Fuchs
        manuscripts
Fuchs
        by place: Altenbergen - Kreuznach


Fuchs ----------------------------------------------------- 1799866
        by place: Langenschwalbach - Zwickau
Fuxbecker - v. Habsburg
Hagen
        manuscripts: Aachen - Himmelspforten


Hagen ----------------------------------------------------- 1799867
        manuscripts: Himmelsmark - Zwätzen b. Jena
Hagen
        by place: Aachen - Minden


Hagen ----------------------------------------------------- 1799868
        by place: Mittweida - Zwätzen b. Jena
Hakale - Hackländer
Hagemann
        manuscripts: Adorf b. Waldeck - Melle


Hagemann -------------------------------------------------- 1799869
        manuscripts: Mengen - Zybien b. Peddenberg
Hegemann
        by place
Haggenmiller - Haltmann


Haltmeyer - Hamelton -------------------------------------- 1799870
Hammer
        manuscripts
Hammer
        by place: Arras - Eilendorf


Hammer ---------------------------------------------------- 1799871
        by place: Frankfurt a/M - Zwickau
Hamerspach - Haüsler
Hahn
        manuscripts
Hahn
        by place: Adersbach - Ehrenberg


Hahn ------------------------------------------------------ 1799872
        by place: Elsfeld - Zwickau
Hanna - Hanow

Hanofsky - Harbrinck -------------------------------------- 1799873


Harbrücker - v. Hartfer ----------------------------------- 1799874
Hartwig
        manuscripts
Hartwig
        by place: Anklam - Weigsdorf
```

```
Hartwig - Hartschke ----------------------------------- 1799875
Hartmann
        manuscripts
Hartmann
        by place: Albersroda - Mühlhausen


Hartmann ---------------------------------------------- 1799322
        by place: Neustadt a/ Orla - Zellerfeld
v. Hartmannsdorf - Karling
Harm(en)s(en)(t)
        manuscripts
Marm(en)s(en)(t)
        by place: Admannshagen - Bad Doberau


Harm(en)s(en)(t) -------------------------------------- 1799323
        by place: Bergedorf - Woguard
v. Harmating - Harzmann
Hase
        manuscripts
Hase
        by place: Albisheim - Bärwalde


Hase -------------------------------------------------- 1799324
        by place: Belgard - Zschopan
Habel - Hannss


v. Haslach - Haugenzeck ------------------------------- 1799325


v. Haugwitz - Hausloth -------------------------------- 1799326
Hausmann
        manuscripts
Hausmann
        by place: Asselfingen - Güstan


Hausmann ---------------------------------------------- 1799351
        by place: Neu-Haldensleben - Zwickau
Haussmüller - Heckenbücher
Hecht
        manuscripts


Hecht ------------------------------------------------- 1799352
        by place
Hechtenberg - Hethfeld


Hethfeld (cont.) - Heigster --------------------------- 1799353
Heide
        manuscripts
Heide
        by place: Aidlingen - Blankenburg
```

```
Heide -------------------------------------------------- 1799354
     by place: Bocken, Klein- - Ziegenhain
Heidacker, Heidecker - Heidorn
Heidenreich
     manuscripts
Heidenreich
     by place: Apolda - Türpitz


Heydenreich -------------------------------------------- 1799355
     by place: Gross Waltersdorf - Zütphen
Heiterer - Heymach,Heimack
Heumann
     manuscripts
Heumann
     by place: Ammelsdorf - Schmöllen


Heimann ------------------------------------------------ 1799356
     by place: Kl. Thiemau - Zehden
Heimar(t) - Haymundt
Hein(e)
     manuscripts
Hein(e)
     by place: Altenburg - Cruela


Hein(e) ------------------------------------------------ 1799357
     by place: Lahde - Züllichau
v. Heinach - Heinold
Heinrich, Henrich, Hinrich, etc.
     manuscripts: Aachen - Halberstadt


Heinrich, etc. ----------------------------------------- 1799358
     manuscripts: Haldensleben - Zyfflich
Heinrich, etc.
     by place
Heinrichsbauer - Heinsohn


Heunsohn  (cont.) - Heinsow ---------------------------- 1799359
Heinz
     manuscripts
Heinz
     by place: Altona  - Lübeck


Heinz -------------------------------------------------- 1799360
     by place: Lüneburg - Zweibrücken
v. Heintzenberg - Heizmann
Hell
     manuscripts: Albeck - Hagen


Hell --------------------------------------------------- 1799361
     manuscripts: Heldensleben - Bärenhausen ?
Hell
     by place
Hehl - Hehleis
Heller
     manuscripts
```

```
Heller ------------------------------------------------------ 1799361
        by place: Algersdorf - Stuttgart


Heller ------------------------------------------------------ 1799362
        by place: Villingen - Wien (Vienna)
Hellerbarth - Helmbold


Helmbrecht - Hemlein ---------------------------------------- 1799363


Hemmelin - Hähner ------------------------------------------- 1799364


Henner  (cont.) - Heniart, Hengart -------------------------- 1799365
Hennig, Henning, Henke
        manuscripts
Hennig, etc.
        by place: Alstedt - Gessing


Heinke - Henscheid ------------------------------------------ 1799213
Henschel
        manuscripts


Henschel ---------------------------------------------------- 1799214
        by place
Henscher - v. Herberstein


v. Herberstein  (cont.) - Herdegen -------------------------- 1799215
Hertel, Hartel
        manuscripts
Hertel, etc.
        by place: Adorf - Joditz


Hertel, etc. ------------------------------------------------ 1799216
        by place: Kahla - Zwickau
Herdenius - de Herimas
Hering, Hörich
        manuscripts
Hering, etc.
        by place: Baumgarten - Prettin


Hering, etc. ------------------------------------------------ 1799217
        by place: Renhardtsdorf - Wiederau
Heringa - Herman
Hermann, Hermanni, Hermanns
        manuscripts
Hermann, etc.
        by place: Berlin - Bockau


Hermann ----------------------------------------------------- 1799218
        by place: Borchhausen - Zwickau
v. Hermannsgrün - Herodes
Herold
        manuscripts: Abtei - Truschnitz


                             29
```

```
Herold ------------------------------------------------------ 1799219
      manuscripts: Thrusing - Zwickau
Herold
      by place
v. Heroldseck - Herzung
Hesse
      manuscripts: Aachen - Gabel (Czechoslovakia)


Hesse ------------------------------------------------------- 1799220
      manuscripts: Gärten - Zwischenahn
Hesse
      by place
Hessart - Hesterkamp


Hestermann - Heuel ----------------------------------------- 1799221
Heuer, Hoyer
      manuscripts
Heuer, etc.
      by place: Ahr - Marieney


Heuer, etc. ------------------------------------------------ 1799222
      by place: Meyen - Zeitz
Heuerhusen - Haecx


v. Hexenagger - Hildbold ----------------------------------- 1799204
Hildebrand(t)
      manuscripts: Adorf - Salbke


Hildebrand(t) ---------------------------------------------- 1799205
      manuscripts: Salzbrunn, Ober- - Zwönitz
Hildebrand(t)
      by place
Hildbrecht - Hillmann


Hillmann  (cont.) - Hinzelmann --------------------------- 1799206
                                                             item 1

Hiop - v. Ho(hen)astenberg ------------------------------ 1797917
Hopp(e)
      manuscripts: Altdamm - Schaarl


Hopp(e) ---------------------------------------------------- 1797717
      manuscripts: Schleessel - Zwilipp
Hopp(e)
      by place
Hoppach - v. Hoberg


v. Hochstetter - Häfele ------------------------------------ 1797718
Hoefer, Hofert, Hopert, Hüfer
      manuscripts: Abtsgmünd - Brüel
```

```
Hoefer, etc.  ----------------------------------------------- 1797719
        manuscripts: Buckau - Fassing
Hofkirchen - Hofet
Hofmann
        manuscripts: Aaberg - Hindenburg


Hofmann -------------------------------------------------- 1797720
        manuscripts: Hirschberg - Zwickau
Hofmann
        by place: Allstedt - Heimitz


Hofmann -------------------------------------------------- 1797721
        by place: Leipzig - Zwickau


Hofmann -------------------------------------------------- 1799712
    Ortsregister zu den verbrannten Karteikarten, 1945     item 4


v. Hofmannsthal - Hoefnagel --------------------------- 1797721
Hoefner, Heppner, Heeffner
        manuscripts
Hoefner, etc.
        by place: Barsinghausen - Repplin


Hoeppner, etc.  ------------------------------------------ 1797722
        by place: Reval - Würtzburg
Häfner - Hölenius
Hol(l)er(ts), Höhler
        manuscripts: Ackeboe - Frankfurt a. M.


Hol(l)er(ts), etc.  -------------------------------------- 1797723
        manuscripts: Freiberg - Zwickau
Hol(l)er(ts), etc.
        by place
Hollermann - Holluschka
Hol(l)z, Holtze(n)
        manuscripts

Hol(l)z, etc.  ------------------------------------------- 1797724
        by place
Holzach - Höhme
Höm(m)an(n)
        manuscripts
Höm(m)an(n)
        by place: Aschersleben - Gottingen


Hom(m)an(n) --------------------------------------------- 1797725
        by place: Hamburg - Werkleitz
Hompeln - Horback


Horbadt - Hormuth --------------------------------------- 1797736
Horn
        manuscripts
Horn
        by place: Altheim - Reilos


                            31
```

```
Horn ------------------------------------------------------- 1797737
       by place: Schönberg - Zwickau
Hornauer - Horstrup


Hörsel - Hupenius ----------------------------------------- 1797738
Huber
       manuscripts
Huber
       by place: Äsch - Hilsbach


Huber ----------------------------------------------------- 1797739
       by place: Hirshwald - Wyl
Huppertsberg - Hubendschuder
Huge, Huch, Hugo
       manuscripts: Aachen - Sandow


Huge, etc. ------------------------------------------------ 1797740
       manuscripts: Schaaken - Zurich
Huge, etc.
       by place
Hugare - Hüttig


Hüttner - Humser ------------------------------------------ 1797741
Huhn, Hühne
       manuscripts: Aahoff - Umkirch


Huhn, etc. ------------------------------------------------ 1797742
       manuscripts: Volckmai - Zorge Harz
Huhn, etc.
       by place
v. Hunawiler- Hüsing


Hüsing(er)  (cont.) - Hyan ------------------------------- 1797743
Ja - Jackow                                                    item 1
Jakob, Jacobi, Jacobsen
       manuscripts
Jakob, etc.
       by place: Aachen - Leipzig


Jakob, etc. ----------------------------------------------- 1797744
       by place: Lengenfeld - Zwickau
Jacobsch - Jamrowski
Jahn, Jansen, Jantzen
       manuscripts
Jahn, etc.
       by place: Abbendorf


Jahn, etc. ------------------------------------------------ 1797745
       by place: Adensen - Zwickau
Jani - Jauch
```

```
Jauchensteiner - Jecht ---------------------------------- 1797860
Jäger
        manuscripts
Jäger
        by place: Aldingen - Markneukirchen


Jäger ------------------------------------------------- 1797861
        by place: Mövs - Witzleben
v. Jägersdorf - Jancke


Jancke  (cont.) - Jeschal ------------------------------ 1797862
Jeschke
        manuscripts
Jeschke
        by place: Bromberg - Pemperstin


Jeschke ------------------------------------------------ 1797863
        by place: Radzye - Züllichau
Jetschick - Ingold


Ingolstädter - Iommer ---------------------------------- 1797864
John
        manuscripts
John
        by place: Alversum - Lichtenau


John --------------------------------------------------- 1797865
        by place: Militsch - Warnsdorf
Jonack - Junack
Jung
        manuscripts: Aachen - Halberstadt


Jung --------------------------------------------------- 1797866
        manuscripts: Halle - Zwickau
Jung
        by place


Jung --------------------------------------------------- 1799712
    by place Nachtrag                                     item 1


Junganders - Jungfer ----------------------------------- 1797866


Jungwirth - Izstein ------------------------------------ 1797867
                                                          item 1

Jüten -------------------------------------------------- 1799712
    by place: Berga - Soest                               item 2


Kapp - Caletinger -------------------------------------- 1799206
Kappel, Kapel, Capelle, Gabel                             item 2
        manuscripts
Kappel, etc.
        by place: Aalborg, Denmark - Hamburg
```

Kappel, etc. -- 1799207
        by place: Konstanz - Wintzingerode
v. der Capelle - Katherberg

Katert - Gallasch ----------------------------------- 1799208

Gallasch (cont.) - Cammana -------------------------- 1799209
Kamp
        manuscripts: Aachen - Gartzweiler

Kamp -- 1799210
        manuscripts: Geldern - Zirne
Kamp
        by place
Gambach - Kantel

v. Kandelau - Carbuhn ------------------------------- 1799211
Karch, Karge, Garecke
        manuscripts: Albertsdorf - Wriezen

Karch, etc. --- 1799212
        manuscripts: Zwickau - Zweibrücken
Karch, etc.
        by place
Gargan - Karsten
Karst
        manuscripts: Ahrenviöl - Bargum

Karst --- 1799223
        manuscripts: Barleben - Zwingenberg
Karst
        by place
Karstens - Gasterstädt

Gasthauer - Kaufenstein ----------------------------- 1799236
Kaul, Kaull, Gaul, Gauhl
        manuscripts: Affalterthal - Herzberg

Kaul, etc. -- 1799237
        manuscripts: Innsbruck - Zwickau
Kaul, etc.
        by place
Kaulbach - Gebwiler
Gebhard(i), Gebert, Geppart, Goepfert
        manuscripts: Abbessen - Müglenz

Gebhard(i), etc. ------------------------------------ 1799238
        manuscripts: Mühlau - Zwönitz

Gebhard(i), etc.
        by place
Kegel
        manuscripts: Aachen - Bayreuth

34

```
Kegel ----------------------------------------------------- 1799239
        manuscripts: Belzig - Zschortau
Kegel
        by place
Kegelmann - Gaibald
Geibel
        manuscripts: Achern - Eger


Geibel ----------------------------------------------------- 1799240
        manuscripts: Elbogen - Wolfshagen
Geibel
        by place
Keiper - Geifrig, Geibrich
Geil, Keil
        manuscripts: Aachen - Poll


Keil ----------------------------------------------------- 1799241
        manuscripts: Parchwitz - Zweimen
Keil
        by place
Keilpflug - Geysenhofer
Kaiser, Keiser, Geisser, Ceasar
        manuscripts: Aachen - Bonn


Keiser, etc. ----------------------------------------------- 1799242
        manuscripts: Borken - Zweimen
Keiser, etc.
        by place
v. Kaisersberg - Geysing
Geissler, Keyssler, Giessler
        manuscripts: Abberode - Frankenhausen


Geisler, etc. ---------------------------------------------- 1799243
        manuscripts: Frankenstein - Zwolno
Geisler, etc.
        by place
Geislinger - Geelvink


Geelvink  (cont.) - Gmeinwieser ---------------------------- 1799244


Gemeinhard - Genzel ---------------------------------------- 1799245


Kentzelmann - Georgonne ------------------------------------ 1799224
Gehr, Kehr
        manuscripts
Gehr, etc.
        by place: Aspach - Frauensee


Gehr, etc. ------------------------------------------------- 1799225
        by place: Hamburg - Kolknitz
Kehren - Gerbst
Gerk, Gericke, Goericke, Girke
        manuscripts
```

Gerk, etc. -- 1799225
        by place: Aspe - Hannover

Gerk, etc. -- 1799226
        by place: Hildesheim - Zerbst
Kerkdorp - Gertmann
Gärtner, Gartner
        manuscripts: Ahrweiller - Weißburg

Gärtner, etc. --- 1799227
        by place: Wiessa - Z.
Gerdom - Kördle
Gerlach
        manuscripts
Gerlach
        by place: Berbersdorf - Kerzdorf

Gerlach --- 1799228
        by place: Crivitz - Zweibrücken
Gerland - Kerstan
Gerstenberg(er), -ber
        manuscripts: Aitzendorf

Gerstenberg(er), -ber --------------------------------------- 1799229
        manuscripts: Altenbürg - Zschoppelshain
Gerstenbrand - Gerstermann
Kestner, Kästner, Kastner
        manuscripts
Kestner, etc.
        by place: Alkersleben - Nöda

Kestner, etc. --- 1799230
        by place: Pretschendorf - Wöllnau
Gestöttner - Geukler

Geugelin - Kieteibl --- 1799231

Küttel - Kind --- 1799232

Kind (cont.) - Kirchmess ----------------------------------- 1799233
Kirchner
        manuscripts: Allendorf - Kamenz

Kirchner -- 1799287
        manuscripts: Karlsruhe - Züllichau
Kirchner
        by place
Kirchniawy - Kirchstein
Kirsten, Kersten, Kürsten
        manuscripts
Kirsten, etc.
        by place: Alkersleben - Breslau

Kirsten, etc. --- 1799288
      by place: Burliebenau - Zschaschelwitz
Cirstenberger - Giesewell

Giesenfeld - Klehr -- 1799289

Claar - Glauning -- 1799290
Claus
      manuscripts: Aachen - Unterhaun

Claus --- 1799291
      manuscripts: Hauptstuhl - Zwönitz
Claus
      by place: Amsterdan - Schmölln

Klaus --- 1799292
      by place: Stahlberg - Zwingenberg
Klausberger - Gleimenhain
Klein
      manuscripts: Aachen - Wichlinghausen

Klein --- 1799293
      manuscripts: Widdersroda - Züsch
Klein
      by place
Kleinadel - Gleisle

Gleisler - Gleu -- 1799294

Kleuber - Gleiss, Kleiss ----------------------------------- 1799295

Glissenberg - Glorius -------------------------------------- 1799296

Glörich - Chlubus -- 1799297
Klug(e), Glück
      manuscripts: Aachen - Seiffenbach, Ober

Klug, etc. --- 1799298
      manuscripts: Seligenstadt - Zwöchau
Klug, etc.
      by place
v. Gluchau - Knabe

Knappe (cont.) - Knizinger --------------------------------- 1799299

Knop, Knopf, Knauks -- 1799300
      manuscripts
Knop
      by place
Knopadel - Conard

```
Knoll ------------------------------------------------------ 1799300
      manuscripts
Knoll
      by place: Ansbach - Mittweida


Knoll ------------------------------------------------------ 1799301
      by place: Neudek - Wolfenbüttel
Knölcke - Gnutzmann
Kopp, Kopf, Köppen, Cöpe
      manuscripts


Kopp, etc. ------------------------------------------------- 1799302
      by place
Kopaniarska - Coppai(s)
Göbel, Goebel, Göbbelt, Kobel
      manuscripts
Göbel, etc.
      by place: Abterode - Krippitz


Göbel, etc. ------------------------------------------------ 1799303
      by place: Lahr - Ziegenhain
Köplmayer - Kobusch
Koch, Cook
      manuscripts: Aalen - Lüdermünd


Koch ------------------------------------------------------- 1799304
      manuscripts
Koch
      by place: Aalen - Lemkendorf


Koch ------------------------------------------------------- 1799305
      by place: Lermoos - Zweibrücken
Koč(z)ka - Koc(z)ur
Godde, Goethe, Kothe, Köthen
      manuscripts: Aachen - Koerbelitz


Godde, etc. ------------------------------------------------ 1799306
      manuscripts: Köslin - Zwickau
Godde, etc.
      by place
Kollak, Kokak - Gottheil

Kotelmann - Coiquaud -------------------------------------- 1799307
Kohl, Golle, Köllen, Göhle
      manuscripts: Aachen - Kirchrath (Netherlands)


Kohl ------------------------------------------------------- 1799308
      manuscripts: Kirspenich - Zwönitz
Kohl
      by place
Kollak - v. Colatzki
Kolbe, Kulpe
      manuscripts
Kolbe, etc.
      by place: Aschersleben - Windsbach
```

```
Kolbe, etc. ------------------------------------------------- 1799309
        by place: Zimmern - Znaim
v. Collenbach - Golentz
Keller, Gellert, Gehler, Köhler, Colar, etc.
        manuscripts: Aachen - Kesselsdorf


Keller, etc. ------------------------------------------------ 1799310
        manuscripts: Charlottenburg - Zwönitz
Keller, etc.
        by place: Alsfeld - Essel


Köhler, etc. ------------------------------------------------ 1799311
        by place: Fleisbach - Stuttgart


Keller, etc. ------------------------------------------------ 1799312
        by place: Talheim - Zwickau
Gollershofer - v. Goltz


v. Goltz (cont.) - Kornhorst -------------------------------- 1799313
König, Köning
        manuscripts: Aach - Staffelstein


König, etc. ------------------------------------------------- 1799314
        manuscripts: Staffelstein - Zwickau
König, etc.
        by place
Koninx - Könemann, etc.


Konopa - Körtgen -------------------------------------------- 1799315


Corte - Körnchen -------------------------------------------- 1799316


Korndörfer - Korbrock --------------------------------------- 1799317
Coss, Goos(sen), Coes, Koss
        manuscripts: Aken - Breckerfeld


Coss, etc. -------------------------------------------------- 1799318
        manuscripts: Breitenau - Zweibrücken
Coss, etc.
        by place
Cosak - Costenoble
Köster, Küster
        manuscripts: Ackenhausen - Lüneburg


Köster, etc. ------------------------------------------------ 1799319
        manuscripts: Lünen - Zweibrücken
Köster
        by place
Cösterbarier - Coyet
Götze(n), Kotze
        manuscripts: Aachen - Crimmitsschau
```

Götze(n), etc. --- 1799320
        manuscripts: Crock - Zwickau
Götze(n)
        by place
Kozak, Kosak - Grabau

Grabau (cont.) - Graerds ------------------------------- 1799321
Graf, Grave, Graife, Greff
        manuscripts

Graf --- 1799656
        by place
Gravack - Kraffczyk
Kraft
        manuscripts
Kraft
        by place: Berlin - Ohrdruf

Kraft -- 1799657
        by place: Röppisch - Witzenhausen
Kraffthal - Grammelstörp
Kramer
        manuscripts: Aachen - Schwersenz

Kramer --- 1799658
        manuscripts: Schwieberdingen - Zwickau
Kramer
        by place
Gramerstetter - v. Cramon

v. Grammont - Graudegus -------------------------------- 1799659

Krauter - Graurock ------------------------------------- 1799660
Krause, Kruse, Crusius
        manuscripts: Aalen - Norenberg

Krause, etc. --- 1799661
        manuscripts: Wieseth - Zwönitz
Krause
        by place: Affalter - Tiefenthal

Krause, etc. --- 1799662
        by place:Tinz - Zwickau
Krauspe - v. Krachnitz
Gregor(y), Gregorius, Greger
        manuscripts: Alkmaas - Altona

Gregor(y), etc. -- 1799663
        manuscripts: Ammensleben - Zwönitz
Gregor(y), etc.
        by place
Gregorck - Greiner

```
Greiner   (cont.) - de Crequier ------------------------- 1799664
Kress
     manuscripts
Kress
     by place: Arnsberg - Göhren


Kress -------------------------------------------------- 1799665
     by place: Halle - Wertheim
Krespach - Kreuseler


Kreuser - Grillo --------------------------------------- 1799666
Grimm
     manuscripts: Adorf - Alsfeld


Grimm -------------------------------------------------- 1799667
     manuscripts; Altenburg - Zwoschnitz
Grimm
     by place
Griemann - Christhold
Christiansen, Christiani
     manuscripts: Aalborg - Berlin


Christiansen, etc. ------------------------------------- 1799668
     manuscripts: Bevertaft - Zwenkau
Christiansen, etc.
     by place
Christianus - v. Kroge


Krokowski - Kromüller ---------------------------------- 1799669
Krohn
     manuscripts: Aachen - Schmelsin


Krohn -------------------------------------------------- 1799670
     manuscripts: Schnelsen - Zwickau
Krohn
     by place
Kronach - Kreher
Gross, Grothe
     manuscripts: Aachen - Weißenfels


Gross, etc. -------------------------------------------- 1799671
     manuscripts: Weißkirchen - Zwönitz
Gross, etc.
     by place
Grosch, Krötzsch, Gretsch
     manuscripts
Grosch, etc.
     by place: Berlin - Kitzingen


Grosch ------------------------------------------------- 1799672
     by place: Langendorf - Werben
Kroitzsch - Grötzner
Grube
     manuscripts
```

```
Grube ---------------------------------------------------- 1799672
        by place: Altenroda - Hannover


Grupe ---------------------------------------------------- 1799673
        by place: Harburg - Vorrade
Gruber - Kriegel
Krüger, Kröger, Krieger
        manuscripts: Abbendorf - Neumarkt


Krüger, etc. --------------------------------------------- 1799674
        manuscripts: Neundorf, Groß- - Zwotzen
Krüger,etc.
        by place: Bardenitz - Uelzen


Krüger, etc. --------------------------------------------- 1799675
        by place: Valle - Zschopau
Krugerke - Gründ


Gründ  (cont.) - Krätner --------------------------------- 1799698
Grünwald, Grienwald
        manuscripts
Grünwald, etc.
        by place: Armstorf - Culmitzsh


Grünewald, etc. ------------------------------------------ 1799699
        by place: Leipzig - Zinten
Grünenwalder - Kupbisch
Kuch(en)
        manuscripts: Aachen - Wittingen


Kuch(en) ------------------------------------------------- 1799700
        manuscripts: Wollin - Zschockau
Kuch(en)
        by place
Kuckartz - Gutkium


Gutgemann - Guizetti ------------------------------------- 1799701
Kuhl
        manuscripts: Aalen - Niedersaathen


Kuhl ----------------------------------------------------- 1799702
        manuscripts: Sachsenhausen - Zwiehalten
Kuhl
        by place
Kukla - Kumeth
Kümmel
        manuscripts
Kümmel
        by place: Asbach - Bothenheilingen
```

```
Kümmel -------------------------------------------------- 1799703
        by place: Delitzsch - Wittenberg
Kümmelberg - Gumz
Kühn, Kien, Kuno
        manuscripts: Aach - Walthersdorf


Kühn, etc. ---------------------------------------------- 1799704
        manuscripts: Wanlo - Zwickau
Kühn, etc.
        by place: Arnstadt - Töpeln


Kühn, etc. ---------------------------------------------- 1799705
        by place: Treptow - Zwickau
v. Guna - Guntelmeyn
Günther
        manuscripts


Günther ------------------------------------------------- 1799706
        by place
Kundert - Günebrainer
Kühnel
        manuscripts


Kühnel -------------------------------------------------- 1799707
        by place
Kunert - Cuni
Künz, Konz
        manuscripts


Künz ---------------------------------------------------- 1799708
        by place
Kunzel - Kurr


Kuhr  (cont.) - Kurszalle ------------------------------- 1799709
Kurtz, Kurth, Korte, Cordes, Curtius
        manuscripts
        by place: Berlstedt - Harelberg

Kurtz, Kurth, Korte, Cordes, Curtius ------------------- 1799710
        by place: Helmstedt - Ziesar

v. Lah -------------------------------------------------- 1797867
Lappe                                                       item 2
        manuscripts: Allendorf - Villigst


Lappe --------------------------------------------------- 1797868
        manuscripts: Vockenhagen - Zimdarse
Lappe
        by place
Laabs - Lammatsch
Lampe
        manuscripts
Lampe
        by place: Bobritzsch - Nördlingen
```

```
Lampe ------------------------------------------------------- 1797869
     by place: Pretzschendorf - Zennern
v. Lamback - de Lannay

Lang
     manuscripts: Absdorf - Cottbus


Lang -------------------------------------------------------- 1797846
     manuscripts: Kotzau - Zwolle
Lang
     by place: Allendorf - Geringswalde


Lang -------------------------------------------------------- 1797847
     by place: Glats - Zwickau
Langacker - Langbein


Langenberg - Landknecht ------------------------------------- 1797848
Landgraf
     manuscripts: Affalter - Willmars


Landgraf ---------------------------------------------------- 1797849
     manuscripts: Winkel (Netherlands) - Zwickau
Landgraf
     by place
Landgrebe - Laubach


v. Laubgassen - Leeborn ------------------------------------- 1797850


Lebrecht - Lemai(t)re --------------------------------------- 1797851
Lehmann
     manuscripts: Adenau - Seuftenberg


Lehmann ----------------------------------------------------- 1797852
     manuscripts: Seyde - Zwietow
Lehmann
     by place
Lehmanski - Lembzer
Lemke
     manuscripts: Alferde - Korbach


Lemke ------------------------------------------------------- 1797853
     manuscripts: Cotwingen - Zielen
Lemke
     by place
Lembcken - Le(h)munger
Lentz, Lantz
     manuscripts: Adolphseck - Aub


Lenz -------------------------------------------------------- 1797854
     manuscripts: Aurich - Zwischenahn
Lenz
     by place
v. Lenzberg - Leopold
```

```
Liebhold - Lesker ------------------------------------------------ 1797855


Lescher - v. Liaukama -------------------------------------------- 1797836
Lieb
      manuscripts


Lieb ------------------------------------------------------------- 1797837
      by place
Liepe - Lipproß


Lips - Lienekampf ------------------------------------------------ 1797838
Linke
      manuscripts: Aachen - Neumunster


Linke ------------------------------------------------------------ 1797839
      manuscripts: Neustadt - Zwenkau
Linke
      by place
Lincka - Linder

Lindner - Lindenau (Nachtrag) ----------------------------------- 1799710
                                                            item 2-3

Linderbeck - Liquestedt ------------------------------------------ 1797840
Lier
      manuscripts
Lier
      by place: Altona - Schwarzfeld


Lier ------------------------------------------------------------- 1797841
      by place: Schwiebus - Züllichau
Lirche - v. Lobdeburg
Lobeck
      manuscripts


Lobeck ----------------------------------------------------------- 1797842
      by place
Loberg - Lodel
Loder
      manuscripts
Loder
      by place: Augsburg - Wersen


Loder ------------------------------------------------------------ 1797843
      by place: Wersen - Zimmern
Lederhose - Loewig


Löffelhad - Lohrengel -------------------------------------------- 1797844


Lorenz, Laurenz -------------------------------------------------- 1797845
      manuscripts
Lorenz, etc.
      by place: Adelby - Thalheim
```

```
Lorenz ------------------------------------------------------ 1797856
        by place: Treptow - Zwönitz
Lorenscraitis - Losebüchel
Losch, Lesch, Löschke
        manuscripts: Altdorf - Stadtamhof


Losch, etc. ------------------------------------------------- 1797857
        manuscripts: Stahnsdorf - Zwickau
Losch, etc.
        by place
Leischke - Loyson
Lotz
        manuscripts
Lotz
        by place: Altenstädten - Altensteig


Lutz -------------------------------------------------------- 1797858
        by place: Augsburg - Zwergen
Lotzbeck - Lubo(w)
Lübke, Lüpke, Lüpkes, Löbbecke, Lipke
        manuscripts
Lübke, etc.
        by place: Bülstringen - Walsborn


Lübke, etc. ------------------------------------------------- 1797859
        by place: Zernenkow
Lübeck - Lükesch


Luckenwald - Lüdel ------------------------------------------ 1798333
Lutter, Lueders
        manuscripts: Achtelsbach - Dargitz


Lutter, etc. ------------------------------------------------ 1798388
        manuscripts: Delitzsch - Zingst
Lutter, etc.
        by place
Luterbach - Lutterotti
Ludwig
        manuscripts


Ludwig ------------------------------------------------------ 1798389
   by place
(v.) Ludwiger - Lungwitz


Lunghort - Macktanz ----------------------------------------- 1798390


Magdeburg - Makerzowsky ------------------------------------- 1798391
Mathes, Matthias, Mattheus, Matthies
        manuscripts: Aachen - Kelsterbach
```

```
Mathes, Matthias, Mattheus, Matthies --------------------- 1798392
    manuscripts: Kemberg - Zwickau
Mathes, Matthias, Mattheus, Matthies
   by place
Matthaei - Matweis


Mattfeld - Mameron ------------------------------------ 1798393
Mann
   manuscripts
Mann
   by place: Pachim in Grabow - Heubach


Mann ------------------------------------------------- 1798394
      by place: Hirschladen - Zellerfeld
Manna(e)rt - Manz(ius)


Mantzke - Marticke ----------------------------------- 1798395
Martin, Mertens
      manuscripts: Aachen - Wanzlitz


Martin, etc. ----------------------------------------- 1798396
      manuscripts: Wardenburg - Zwönitz
Martin, etc.
      by place: Alsfeld - Zwickau
Marting - Marels


Marencke - Marutzke ---------------------------------- 1798397
Marx
      manuscripts: Aachen - Coswig


Marx ------------------------------------------------- 1798398
      manuscripts: Coswig - Zwickau
v. Marxheim - Masterton


Masuch - Maaz ---------------------------------------- 1798399


Matzen - v. Mchun ------------------------------------ 1798400
May, etc.
      manuscripts: Aahof - Kreuznach


May, etc. -------------------------------------------- 1798401
      manuscripts: Krotzenburg - Zweibrücken
May, etc.
      by place
Maybach - Meinreis
Meier
      manuscripts: Aachen - Detmold


Meier ------------------------------------------------ 1798402
      manuscripts: Deufringen - Schlat
```

```
Meier -------------------------------------------------------- 1798403
        manuscripts: Schledehausen - Zwönitz
Meier
        by place: Belgard - Farven


Meier -------------------------------------------------------- 1798404
        by place: Farwick - Rhoden


Meier -------------------------------------------------------- 1798405
        by place: Riedmühlen - Zweibrücken
Meieran - Maierbusch
Meincke. Meinecke
        manuscripts
Meincke, etc.
        by place: Apeusen - Seedorf


Meincke, etc. ------------------------------------------------ 1798406
        by place: Strüssendorf - Westerhusen
Meinekat - Maystetter
Meister
        manuscripts: Adolphhausen - Schonigen


Meister ------------------------------------------------------ 1798470
        manuscripts: Schramtal - Zwickau
Meister
        by place
Meisterknecht - Meldendorf


Meletta - Memmert -------------------------------------------- 1798471
Menke
        manuscripts
Menke
        by place: Berzahn - Wettelswalde


Menke -------------------------------------------------------- 1798472
        by place: Wolfenbüttel
Männichen - Mentzendorf
Menzel
        manuscripts
Menzel
        by place: Breslau - Langenbielau


Menzel ------------------------------------------------------- 1798473
        by place: Magdeburg - Zittau
Menzer- Merkir


Merkisch - Messhammer ---------------------------------------- 1798474


Mesenhol - Matzke -------------------------------------------- 1798475
Metzger
        manuscripts
```

Metzger -- 1798476
        by place
Metztacken - Mikkaitis
Michel
        manuscripts

Michel --- 1798477
        by place
Michelau - Mittlehner

Mittler - Michsler --- 1798478

Mitze - Move --- 1798479

Movitz - Montu --- 1798480
Mönch, Münch
        manuscripts: Aachen - Laubach

Mönch, etc. -- 1798481
        manuscripts: Landa - Zwenkau
Mönch, etc.
        by place
v. Münchhausen - Monzmann
Mohr
        manuscripts: Aachen - Liechtenegg

Mohr --- 1798482
        manuscripts: Limback - Zymna
Mohr
        by place
Morat - Moritzsch
Moritz - Mauritzsch
        manuscripts: Aachen - Mertz (Switzerland)

Moritz --- 1798483
        by place
Morlin - Mossin

de Mosina - Mülberg(er), -i ------------------------------------ 1798484

Mühlbradt - Mühleutz --- 1798485
Müller, Möller
        manuscripts: Altenberg - Harpe

Müller, etc. --- 1798486
        manuscripts: Harrien - Pfühl

Müller, etc. --- 1798487
        manuscripts: Pfüllendorf - Zwötzen

Müller, etc. --- 1798488
        by place: Ablass - Diesdorf

Müller, etc. --- 1798489
        by place: Dilsberg - Heilbronn

Müller, etc. --- 1798616
        by place: Heilbronn (Kloster) - Marburg

Müller, etc. --- 1798617
        by place: St. Margarethen - Neuruppin

Müller, etc. --- 1798618
        by place: Saalbach - Witzschdorf

Müller, etc. --- 1798619
        by place: Wörlitz - Zwota
Müllerklein - Müntz

Münzel - Nagel --- 1798620

Nagel (Forts.) - Naum --------------------------------------- 1798621
Naumann
        manuscripts
Naumann
        by place: Altenburg - Gersdorf

Naumann -- 1798622
        by place: Gostewitz - Zuschendorf
v. der Naumberg - Neimcke

Naimer - Neupelt --- 1798623
Neubert
        manuscripts: Abtenau - Irfersgrün

Neubert -- 1798624
        manuscripts: Cainsdorf - Zwickau
Neubert
        by place
v. Neuberg - Neuhase
Neuhaus
        manuscripts
Neuhaus
        by place: Barmen - Hildesheim

Neuhaus -- 1798625
        by place: Camen - Viersen
Niehausen - Neum
Neumann, Niemann, Neander
        manuscripts
Neumann, etc.
        by place: Anklam - Kalwe

Neumann, etc. -- 1798626
        by place: Königsburg - Züllichau
v. Neumark - Niekamp

Niekammer - Nielsen --- 1798627

v. Nielande - Niesinger --------------------------------------- 1798628

Nisinsky - Nolber --- 1798629
Nold(a), Noltzen
        manuscripts
Nold(a)
        by place: Groß Almerode - Wolfhagen

Noelke - Obach -- 1798630

v. Opalinsky - v. Oebisfelde ---------------------------------- 1798631
Opitz
        manuscripts: Aga - Diedendorf

Opitz --- 1798632
        manuscripts: Dippoldiswalde - Zwickau
Opitz
        by place: Bischheim -Züllischau
Obladen - Oetner
Otto, Otten
        manuscripts: Abberode - Gröben

Otto, etc. -- 1798633
        manuscripts: Gröditz - Zwönitz
Otto, etc.
        by place: Augsburg - Markneukirchen

Otto, etc. -- 1798634
        by place: Meerholz - Zwickau
Ottofar - v. Oldenburg

Oldenburger - Ölzner -- 1798635
Ohm
        manuscripts
Ohm
        by place

Omann - Ortner -- 1798572

Ordnung - d'Ossery -- 1798573
Oswald
        manuscripts: Aeschi Kanton - Giersdorf

```
Oswald ---------------------------------------------------- 1798574
      manuscripts: Giessen - Zwingenberg
Oswald
      by place
Ossenwarde - Quinger


Quintel - v. Rabenau ------------------------------------- 1798575


v. Rabeneck - Radonsky ----------------------------------- 1798576


Radoezkiv - Ranzow --------------------------------------- 1798577


Ranzenback - Rathkeale ----------------------------------- 1798578
Rau(ch)
      manuscripts
Rauch
      by place: Berstadt - Potsdam


Rau(ch) -------------------------------------------------- 1798579
      by place: Rietschütz - Züllichau
Rauff - v. Räpich


v. Rephun - Redenz --------------------------------------- 1798580


Reder - Reichenauer -------------------------------------- 1798581
Reichenbach
      manuscripts


Reichenbach ---------------------------------------------- 1798582
      by place
Reichenbacher - v. Reigersberg
Reichert, Reichard, etc.
      manuscripts
Reichert, etc.
      by place: Alsfeld - Tharandt


Reicherd, etc. ------------------------------------------- 1798583
      by place: Ulm - Weißenfels
Reuker - Reimel
Reimer
      manuscripts: Ahorn - Lemsal (Latvia)


Reimer --------------------------------------------------- 1798584
      manuscripts: Lensahn - Zitzewitz
Reimer
      by place:
Reiner - Reinstorf
```

Reintorff (cont.) - Reinshagen ------------------------- 1798585
Reinhard
        manuscripts
Reinhard
        by place: Altenburg - Ubach (Netherlands)

Reinhard --- 1798586
        by place: Volkhardinghausen - Zeitz
Reinharz - Reling

Rehlinger - Renns -------------------------------------- 1798587
Rensch, Ronsch, Rinsch, Renisch
        manuscripts
Rensch, etc.
        by place: Buderich - Wölfelsdorf

Renschel - Reutel -------------------------------------- 1798588
Reuter, Reiter
        manuscripts
Reuter, etc.
        by place: Gabelbach - Tiefengruben

Reuter, etc. --- 1798589
        by place: Tübingen - Zwönitz
Reuthershan - Rippner
Reicke
        manuscripts: Abtsgmünd - Kirchensittenbach

Riecke --- 1798590
        manuscripts: Kirchsstuck - Zwolle
Riecke
        by place: Allermöhe - Witthund
Riga - v. Richtenberg
Richter
        manuscripts: Aalenberg - Storkow

Richter -- 1798591
        manuscripts: Strauch - Zwönitz
Richter
        by place: Ablass - Luckau (Netherlands)

Richter -- 1798552
        by place: Lübben - Zwickau
v. Richtergen - Rid

Rieth - Rydenius --------------------------------------- 1798553
Ritter
        manuscripts: Aachen - Wunneschin

```
Ritter ----------------------------------------------------- 1798554
        manuscripts: Wunsiedel - Zwenkau
Ritter
        by place
v. Rittersbach - Rinegrock
Ring
        manuscripts: Achim - Müllendorf


Ring ------------------------------------------------------- 1798555
        manuscripts: Mülheim - Zohlow
Ring
        by place
Rinckart - Rischebusch


Rischenthal - Robrah(n) ------------------------------------ 1798556


Robrecht - Rochus ------------------------------------------ 1798557
Roth
        manuscripts: Aachen - Lennep


Roth ------------------------------------------------------- 1798558
        manuscripts: Lenzen - Zwölzen

Roth
        by place: Adorf - Platten


Roth ------------------------------------------------------- 1798559
        by place: Plauen - Zwickau
v. Roda - Rödelsturz
Rotter, Roeder
        manuscripts


Rotter, etc. ----------------------------------------------- 1798560
        by place
Roterberg - Röist
Roll, Roehl, Rehl
        manuscripts: Akams - Blumenrath


Roll, etc. ------------------------------------------------- 1798561
        manuscripts: Bochum - Zscherben
Roll, etc.
        by place
Rolla du Rosi - da Romano


Romanov - Ronnet ------------------------------------------- 1798562


Röhner - Roos ---------------------------------------------- 1798563


Rosen - Rosenbusch ----------------------------------------- 1798564
Rosch, Resch
        manuscripts
Rosch, etc.
        by place: Baiersdorf - Guben
```

```
Rosch, etc. ------------------------------------------------ 1798565
      by place: St. Johann - Zwochau
Roszka - Rosegger


Rösel - Ruben --------------------------------------------- 1798566


Rub - Ruchholts ------------------------------------------- 1798567
Rueger, Rieger
      manuscripts
Rueger, etc.
      by place: Dresden


Rueger, etc. ---------------------------------------------- 1798568
      by place:
Rickersfelde - v. Rudigsdorf
Ruediger, Roediger, Riediger
      manuscripts
Ruediger, etc.
      by place: Amerback - Köln


Ruediger, etc. -------------------------------------------- 1798569
      by place: Kraftsdorf - Westernhausen
v. Rüdigersdorf - Rudolf


Rudorf - Rünberg ------------------------------------------ 1798570
Runge, Ronge
      manuscripts: Aabenraa - Auvos


Runge, etc. ----------------------------------------------- 1798571
      manuscripts: Bärenwalde - Zottitz
Runge, etc.
      by place: Berlin - Winsdorf
Rungaldier - Rüxleben


Rüxner - Sahliger ----------------------------------------- 1798592


Salici - Santelmann --------------------------------------- 1798593
Sander
      manuscripts
Sander
      by place: Algernissen - Seegeritz

Sander ---------------------------------------------------- 1799525
      by place: Wolfenbüttel - Zickeritz
Sanderskerl - Sandver
Sauer
      manuscripts
Sauer
      by place: Amberg - Erdmannsdorf


Sauer ----------------------------------------------------- 1799526
      by place: Frankfurt - Sondershausen
Suhr - Span(n)(heymer)
```

```
Spohn - Sperlebom ----------------------------------------- 1799527
Sperling
      manuscripts: Annarde - Kamenz


Sperling ------------------------------------------------- 1799528
      manuscripts: Kammin - Zschoch(au)(er)
Sperling
      by place
Spindler - Spring


Springar - v. Spillenberger ----------------------------- 1799529


Spillebout - Scaturigius -------------------------------- 1799530
Schaaf
      manuscripts
Schaaf
      by place: Bennewitz - Landau


Schaaf --------------------------------------------------- 1799531
      by place: Lindenhain - Sindolsheim
Schawacht - Scharren
Scharf, Scharpe
      manuscripts: Appenrode - Lüdenscheid


Scharf --------------------------------------------------- 1799532
      by place: Mulsen - Zierenberg
Scharfenbaum - Scheck


Scheckabura - Scheren(ius) ------------------------------ 1799533
Schaefer, Schoeffer
      manuscripts
Schaefer, etc.
      by place: Altenroda - Dankmarshausen


Schaefer ------------------------------------------------- 1799534
      by place: Danzig - Zweibrucken
Schefferlin - Schehin
Scheibe
      manuscripts
Scheibe
      by place: Altenburg - Wenigenauma


Scheiba - Scheizach -------------------------------------- 1799515
Scheele, Scholl
      manuscripts
Schelle, etc.
      by place: Aachen - Hanau


Scheele -------------------------------------------------- 1799516
      by place: Hannover - Wiesa
Schellan - Schenberg
Schenk
      manuscripts: Abstatt - Leipnitz
```

Schenk -- 1799517
     manuscripts: Leipzig - Zwickau
Schenk
     by place
Schenkenback - Scheremetieff
Scherer
     manuscripts
Scherer
     by place: Betzingen - Hannover

Scherer --- 1799518
     by place: Cassel - Weil
Scherpf - v. Schätzler
Schwab
     manuscripts
Schwab
     by place: Ansbach - Nürnberg

Schwab -- 1799519
     by place: Rebesgrun - Windsheim
Schwabach - v. Schwarse
Schwarz
     manuscripts: Aachen - Wupperfeld

Schwarz --- 1799520
     manuscripts: Würmberg - Zwickau
Schwarz
     by place
v. Schwarzach - v. Schwebda

Schwebel - Schwenkenbecher ---------------------------------- 1799521

Schwenkenbecher (cont.) - Schiett --------------------------- 1799522

Schiede - Schiltel -- 1799523
Schilling, Schelling
     manuscripts

Schilling --- 1799524
     by place
Schillinger - Schier

Tschira - Schlechtleitner ----------------------------------- 1799505
Schlegel
     manuscripts: Aderstedt - Frankfurt/a.O.

Schlegel -- 1799506
     manuscripts: Frauenburg - Zwickau
Schlegel
     by place
Schlegelberger - v. Schlieben

```
v. Schlieben  (cont.) - Schlütgens --------------------- 1799507
Schlüter
       manuscripts: Aachen - Stolzenau


Schlüter --------------------------------------------- 1799508
       manuscripts: Stralsund - Zirzow
Schlüter
       by place
Schlüderberg - Schmicking
Schmidt, Schmitz, Fabricius
       manuscripts: Aachen - Abtsgemünd


Schmidt, etc. --------------------------------------- 1799509
       manuscripts: Abtshagen - Kelbra


Schmidt, etc. --------------------------------------- 1799510
       manuscripts: Celle - Schusseritz


Schmidt, etc. --------------------------------------- 1799511
       manuscripts: Schulenburg - Zwota
Schmidt, etc.
       without place
Schmidt, etc.
       by place: Aachen - Blaubeuren


Schmidt, etc. --------------------------------------- 1799512
       by place: Bobeck - Hannover


Schmidt --------------------------------------------- 1799513
       by place: Hard - Molbis (Switzerland)


Schmidt, etc. --------------------------------------- 1799514
       by place: Momerzheim - Schwiebus


Schmidt --------------------------------------------- 1799838
       by place: Stadthagen - Zwickau
Schmidag - Schmierenbeck


Smirek - Schneidem ---------------------------------- 1799839
Schneider
       manuscripts: Aachen - Hergensweiler


Schneider ------------------------------------------- 1799840
       manuscripts: Hermannsdorf - Zwoschwitz
Schneider
       by place: Ablass - Gera


Schneider ------------------------------------------- 1799841
       by place: Gersdorf - Zöblitz
```

```
Schneider ------------------------------------------------ 1799842
     by place: Zschopau - Zwoschwitz
Schneiderbauer - Schobel
Schober
     manuscripts: Adolzfurt - Frankfurt a/O


Schober -------------------------------------------------- 1799843
     manuscripts: Fürth - Zschochau
Schober
     by place
Schopphoff - Schopf


Schowalter - Schöntur ------------------------------------ 1799844


Schoneck - Schoss ---------------------------------------- 1799845


Schossau  (cont.) - Schraub ------------------------------ 1799846


Schraut - Schreijäckls ----------------------------------- 1799847


Schreivogel - Schrökel ----------------------------------- 1799828
Schröder
     manuscripts: Aachen - Vorsfelde


Schröder ------------------------------------------------- 1799829
     manuscripts: Wadendorf - Zwickau
Schröder
     without place
Schröder
     by place: Alsleben - Ruppin


Schröder ------------------------------------------------- 1799830
     by place: Sachsenhausen - Zwickau
Schrötteringk - Schupper
Schubert, Schubart
     manuscripts
Schubert, etc.
     by place: Bärenstein - Bellmansdorf


Schubert, etc. ------------------------------------------- 1799831
     by place: Blankehain - Zwickau
Schuttäus - Schukraf(t)
Schütte
     manuscripts
Schütte
     by place: Anklam - Frankfurt a/M


Schütte -------------------------------------------------- 1799832
     by place: Burg Friedberg - Zingst
Skuhta - Schueldorf
Schueler, Schiller
     manuscripts
```

```
Schueler, etc.  ------------------------------------------- 1799832
     by place: Alfershausen - Neuendorf


Schueler, etc.  ------------------------------------------- 1799833
     by place: Nürnberg - Züllichau
Schillermann - Sculteten
Schulz(e), Scholz, Schultheiss
     manuscripts: Aarau - Cuppa


Schulz(e), etc.  ------------------------------------------ 1799834
     manuscripts: Cuppa - Zwolla (Netherlands)


Schulz(e), etc.  ------------------------------------------ 1799835
     by place: Altenburg - Gransee


Schulz(e), etc.  ------------------------------------------ 1799836
     by place: Grauenhagen - Ottendorf


Schulz(e), etc.  ------------------------------------------ 1799837
     by place: Paderborn - Zerbst


Schulz(e), etc.  ------------------------------------------ 1799818
     by place: Zethlingen - Züllichau
Schultkehs - Schuhmacher

Schumann
     manuscripts: Aerzen - Wiesa


Schumann  -------------------------------------------------- 1799819
     manuscripts: Wiesenthal - Zwönitz
Schumann
     by place
Schumarts - Schuhschneck
Schuster
     manuscripts: Affalter - Borne


Schuster  -------------------------------------------------- 1799820
     manuscripts: Brachstedt - Zweimen
Schuster
     by place
Schusterbauer - Schusmann
Schütze
     manuscripts
Schutze
     by place: Alsleben - Lauf


Schütze  --------------------------------------------------- 1799821
     by place: Lauffen - Zwickau
Schutzenbach - v. Stahofsky
Stahl
     manuscripts
Stahl
     by place: Ansbach - Gröningen
```

```
Stahl ------------------------------------------------ 1799822
     by place: Heimsheim - Zerbst
Stahel - Starbusch
Starke
     manuscripts
Starke
     by place: Allendorf - Dresden


Starcke ----------------------------------------------- 1799823
     by place: Erfurt - Ziegelberg
Stargardt - Stegkämpers
Steger, Steiger, Stecker
     manuscripts: Affoltern - Berlin-Pankow


Steger, etc. ------------------------------------------ 1799824
     manuscripts: Bern - Zwickau
Steger, etc.
     by place
Stöcker - Stetnisch
Steffan, Steffen
     manuscripts: Aachen - Lembach


Steffen ----------------------------------------------- 1799825
     manuscripts:
Steffen
     by place
Stephansberger - Steimlin
Stein
     manuscripts: Abterode - Mitau (Courland)


Stein ------------------------------------------------- 1799826
     manuscripts: Mocketal - Zwenkau
Stein
     by place
Steinach - Steinbusch


Steinegg - Steinmer ----------------------------------- 1799827
Steinmetz
     manuscripts: Aga - Sebnitz


Steinmetz --------------------------------------------- 1799907
     manuscripts: Speyer - Zwickau
Steinmetz
     by place
Steinmeyer - Sternickel


Steiniger - Stiemann ---------------------------------- 1799908


Stimp - v. Stojentin ---------------------------------- 1799909
Stoll
     manuscripts: Aach - Dörrenback
```

Stoll --- 1799910
        manuscripts: Dötlingen - Zwette
Stoll
        by place
Stölpe - Storch

Storkappen - Strassereuter ---------------------------- 1799911
  Straube, Strube, Struwe
        manuscripts
  Straube, etc.
        by place: Achern - Münder

  Straube, etc. -- 1799912
        by place: Northeim - Wolfenbüttel
  Straubach - Strickel

  Stricker - Stubbe ------------------------------------ 1799913

  Stubbe (cont.) - Sturler ----------------------------- 1799914
  Sturm
        manuscripts
  Sturm
        by place: Allendorf - Kulm

  Sturm -- 1799915
        by place: Magdeburg - Zittau
  Sturmatis - Sewing

  Segefried - Seidenthal ------------------------------- 1799916
  Seidel, Siedel
        manuscripts

  Seidel, etc. --- 1799906
        by place
  Seidelberg - Seiffke
  Seifert, Seifart, Seyfried
        manuscripts: Aachen - Kaiserslautern

  Seifert -- 1799366
        manuscripts: Kaisitz - Zegefried
  Seifert
        by place: Achstedt - Clausnitz

  Seifert -- 1799367
        by place: Köchendorf - Zwönitz
  v. Seyffertitz - Seistler

  Seissel - Sellschopp --------------------------------- 1799368

  v. Sellenstedt - Swisimg ----------------------------- 1799369

```
Switzer - v. Siggem ------------------------------------- 1799370
Siegert
      manuscripts
Siegert
      by place: Arnstadt - Sorau (Netherlands)


Sigharter - v. Simolin --------------------------------- 1799371
Simon
      manuscripts: Aachen - Reichenbach


Simon -------------------------------------------------- 1799372
      manuscripts: Reichenbach - Zwingenberg
Simon
      by place
Simonards - Soop


Soppek - Somelis --------------------------------------- 1799373
Sommer
      manuscripts
Sommer
      by place: Aarau (Switzerland) - Schönau


Sommer ------------------------------------------------- 1799374
      by place: Streumen - Zwickau
Sommerauer - Sutfeld


Suthagen - Uckerath ------------------------------------ 1799375


Uckermann - Uljanow ------------------------------------ 1799376
Ulig, Uhlig
      manuscripts
Ulig, etc.
      by place: Allendorf - Erlbach


Ulig, etc. --------------------------------------------- 1799377
      by place: Frankenberg - Zwickau
Ullickrath - Ulenreuter
Ulrich
      manuscripts
Ulrcih
      by place: Aken - Dörnten


Ulrich ------------------------------------------------- 1799378
      by place: Ebersbrunn - Zwickau
v. Ulssen - Unter-Ecker


Undereick - Zamoyska ----------------------------------- 1799379
Zahn
      manuscripts: Aach - Buckau
```

```
Zahn ----------------------------------------------------- 1799380
      manuscripts: Buchenau - Zwickau
Zahn
      by place
Zanach - Seine


Zeipert - Zernau ----------------------------------------- 1799381


Zernecke - Zeiglgruber ----------------------------------- 1799382


v. Ziegelheim - Zitterkopf -------------------------------- 1799383


Zittermann - Zimmerling ----------------------------------- 1799384
Zimmermann
      manuscripts: Aachen - Schleuringen


Zimmermann ------------------------------------------------ 1799385
      manuscripts: Schlüchtern - Zwötzen
Zimmermann
      by place
Zimmermeyer - Zinnberger
Zinke
      manuscripts: Aachen - Bubikon


Zinke ----------------------------------------------------- 1799234
      manuscripts: Büden - Zschortau
Zinke
      by place
Zinkand - Zohka


Zoephel - Zutzenheimer, Sossenheimer --------------------- 1799235



EINSENDERKARTEI (SUBMITTER CARDS)

Aarden - Eichenauer--------------------------------------- 1798338
v. Eichendorff - Herzog ---------------------------------- 1798339
Herzog  (cont.) - Lindner -------------------------------- 1798340
Lindner  (cont.) - Reinstorf ----------------------------- 1798341
Reise - Stück -------------------------------------------- 1798342
Stueler - Zwirner ---------------------------------------- 1798343
                                                             item 1



AHNENLISTEN-NUMMERNKARTEI (ANCESTOR LISTS BY SUBMISSION NUMBER)

0001-0595 ------------------------------------------------ 1798343
                                                             item 2
0596-3345 ------------------------------------------------ 1798344
3346-6000 ------------------------------------------------ 1798334
6001-9140 ------------------------------------------------ 1798335
9141-11352 ----------------------------------------------- 1798336
```

BERÜHMTENKARTEI (CELEBRITY/NOBILITY INDEX)

Abbe - Zschokke -- 1798337
item 1

ORTSKARTEI (LOCALITY INDEX)

Aachen - Zwickau -- 1798337
item 2

SACHKARTEI (VOCATION AND SUBJECT INDEX)

Apotheker - Zwillinge ------------------------------------ 1798337
item 3

NUMMERNKARTEI (DATA SOURCE CODE CARDS)

A 00001 - A 02170 -- 1798327

A 02171 - A 04774 -- 1798328

A 04775 - A 07058 -- 1798329

A 07059 - A 10930 -- 1798330

A 10931 - A 22584 -- 1798331
item 1
BR 02142 - BR 63144 -------------------------------------- 1798331
item 2
D 00002 - D 00684 -- 1798331
item 3
E 00001 - E 00021 -- 1798332
item 1
F 00001 - F 00689 -- 1798332
item 2
FR 01/42 - F 1348/35 ------------------------------------- 1798332
item 3
N 00001 - N 02178 -- 1798332
item 4-5
R 00001 - R 00202 -- 1798332
item 6
S 00001 - S 00106 -- 1798332
item 7

AHNENTAFELN (AL) MANUSCRIPT NUMBERS
PART II

FILM NUMBER

```
00001-00019 ---------------------------------------------------- 1809152
00020-00043 ---------------------------------------------------- 1809153
00043  (cont.) ------------------------------------------------- 1809154
                                                                  item 1
00044-00054 ---------------------------------------------------- 1767764
00054-00066 ---------------------------------------------------- 1767765
00067-00068 ---------------------------------------------------- 1767766
                                                                  item 1-2
00076 --------------------------------------------------------- 1767766
                                                                  item 3
00078 --------------------------------------------------------- 1767766
                                                                  item 4
00079-00080 ---------------------------------------------------- 1807406
                                                                  item 1-2
00082-00087 ---------------------------------------------------- 1807406
                                                                  item 3-8
00090 --------------------------------------------------------- 1807406
                                                                  item 9
00093-00095 ---------------------------------------------------- 1807406
                                                                  item 10-12
00099-00100 ---------------------------------------------------- 1807406
                                                                  item 13-14
00102-00105 ---------------------------------------------------- 1807406
                                                                  item 15-18
00107 --------------------------------------------------------- 1807406
                                                                  item 19
00109-00110 ---------------------------------------------------- 1807406
                                                                  item 20-21
00114 --------------------------------------------------------- 1807406
                                                                  item 22
00116-00118 ---------------------------------------------------- 1807406
                                                                  item 23-25
00120 --------------------------------------------------------- 1807406
                                                                  item 26
00121 --------------------------------------------------------- 1807406
                                                                  item 27
00122-00123 ---------------------------------------------------- 1807406
                                                                  item 28-29
00125-00126 ---------------------------------------------------- 1807406
                                                                  item 27
00127-00129 ---------------------------------------------------- 1807408
                                                                  item 1-3
00133-00137 ---------------------------------------------------- 1807408
                                                                  item 4-8
00139-00140 ---------------------------------------------------- 1807408
                                                                  item 9-10
00143-00147 ---------------------------------------------------- 1807408
                                                                  item 11-15
00149-00157 ---------------------------------------------------- 1807408
                                                                  item 16-24
00158 --------------------------------------------------------- 1807409
                                                                  item 1
00161-00164 ---------------------------------------------------- 1807409
                                                                  item 2-5
```

```
00166 ------------------------------------------------------- 1807409
                                                         item 6
00168-00171 ------------------------------------------------- 1807409
                                                         item 8-10
00172-00173 ------------------------------------------------- 1767699
                                                         item 1-2
00176-00177 ------------------------------------------------- 1767699
                                                         item 3-4
00179 ------------------------------------------------------- 1767699
                                                         item 5
00181 ------------------------------------------------------- 1767699
                                                         item 6
00183-00186 ------------------------------------------------- 1767699
                                                         item 7-10
00188-00194 ------------------------------------------------- 1767699
                                                         item 11-17
00196-00204 ------------------------------------------------- 1767699
                                                         item 18-22
00205-00208 ------------------------------------------------- 1767700
                                                         item 1-4
00210 ------------------------------------------------------- 1767700
                                                         item 5
00213 ------------------------------------------------------- 1767700
                                                         item 6
00215-00221 ------------------------------------------------- 1767700
                                                         item 7-13
00223-00229 ------------------------------------------------- 1767700
                                                         item 14-20
00231 ------------------------------------------------------- 1767700
                                                         item 21
00233-00234 ------------------------------------------------- 1767700
                                                         item 1
00241-00242 ------------------------------------------------- 1767701
                                                         item 2-3
00244 ------------------------------------------------------- 1767701
                                                         item 4
00247-00248 ------------------------------------------------- 1767701
                                                         item 5-6
00251-00252 ------------------------------------------------- 1767701
                                                         item 7-8
00256 ------------------------------------------------------- 1767701
                                                         item 9
00258-00260 ------------------------------------------------- 1767701
                                                         item 10
00263-00264 ------------------------------------------------- 1767701
                                                         item 11-12
00266 ------------------------------------------------------- 1809132
                                                         item 1
00269-00276 ------------------------------------------------- 1809132
                                                         item 2-7
00278-00282 ------------------------------------------------- 1809132
                                                         item 8-12
00284-00286 ------------------------------------------------- 1809132
                                                         item 13-15
00289-00290 ------------------------------------------------- 1809132
                                                         item 16-17
00291-00296 ------------------------------------------------- 1809134
                                                         item 10-14
00298 ------------------------------------------------------- 1809134
                                                         item 15
00304-00306 ------------------------------------------------- 1809134
                                                         item 16-18
```

```
00308  --------------------------------------------------- 1809134
                                                      item 19
00309  --------------------------------------------------- 1767774
                                                       item 1
00311-00317  --------------------------------------------- 1767774
                                                      item 2-8
00320-00323  --------------------------------------------- 1767774
                                                     item 9-12
00326  --------------------------------------------------- 1767774
                                                      item 13
00330-00335  --------------------------------------------- 1767774
                                                    item 14-19
00337  --------------------------------------------------- 1767774
                                                      item 20
00340  --------------------------------------------------- 1767774
                                                      item 21
00342  --------------------------------------------------- 1767774
                                                      item 22
00345-00348  --------------------------------------------- 1767774
                                                    item 23-26
00354  --------------------------------------------------- 1767774
                                                      item 27
00354-00355  --------------------------------------------- 1767775
                                                     item 1-2
00359-00360  --------------------------------------------- 1767775
                                                     item 3-4
00362-00364  --------------------------------------------- 1767775
                                                     item 5-7
00366  --------------------------------------------------- 1767775
                                                       item 8
00368  --------------------------------------------------- 1767775
                                                       item 9
00369-00373  --------------------------------------------- 1767387
                                                     item 1-4
00375-00380  --------------------------------------------- 1767387
                                                    item 5-10
00383-00388  --------------------------------------------- 1767387
                                                   item 11-16
00389  --------------------------------------------------- 1767388
                                                       item 1
00391-00402  --------------------------------------------- 1767388
                                                    item 2-13
00404-00405  --------------------------------------------- 1767388
                                                   item 14-15
00407  --------------------------------------------------- 1767388
                                                      item 16
00409-00415  --------------------------------------------- 1767388
                                                   item 17-23
00416  --------------------------------------------------- 1809572
                                                       item 1
00418-00424  --------------------------------------------- 1809572
                                                     item 2-8
00431-00432  --------------------------------------------- 1809572
                                                    item 9-10
00435-00437  --------------------------------------------- 1809572
                                                   item 11-13
00438-00440  --------------------------------------------- 1809604
                                                     item 1-3
00442-00449  --------------------------------------------- 1809604
                                                    item 4-11
00451  --------------------------------------------------- 1809604
                                                      item 12
```

```
00453 ------------------------------------------------------- 1809604
                                                         item 13
00455-00456 ------------------------------------------------- 1809604
                                                         item 14-15
00459 ------------------------------------------------------- 1809604
                                                         item 16
00462 ------------------------------------------------------- 1809604
                                                         item 17
00463 ------------------------------------------------------- 1767766
                                                         item 5
00465-00475 ------------------------------------------------- 1767766
                                                         item 6-16
00476 no. 1 ------------------------------------------------- 1767767
00476 no. 1-2 ----------------------------------------------- 1767768
00477 ------------------------------------------------------- 1809154
                                                         item 2
00479 ------------------------------------------------------- 1809154
                                                         item 3
00481 ------------------------------------------------------- 1809154
                                                         item 4
00485-00486 ------------------------------------------------- 1809154
                                                         item 5-6
00490-00491 ------------------------------------------------- 1809154
                                                         item 7-8
00496 ------------------------------------------------------- 1809154
                                                         item 9
00499 ------------------------------------------------------- 1809154
                                                         item 10
00502 ------------------------------------------------------- 1809572
                                                         item 7
00503 ------------------------------------------------------- 1809154
                                                         item 11
00505 ------------------------------------------------------- 1809154
                                                         item 12
00507 ------------------------------------------------------- 1809154
                                                         item 13
00509-00510 ------------------------------------------------- 1809154
                                                         item 14-15
00513-00514 ------------------------------------------------- 1809154
                                                         item 16-17
00517 ------------------------------------------------------- 1809155
                                                         item 1
00519-00520 ------------------------------------------------- 1809155
                                                         item 2-3
00522 ------------------------------------------------------- 1809155
                                                         item 4
00527-00531 ------------------------------------------------- 1809155
                                                         item 5-9
00533-00552 ------------------------------------------------- 1767769
                                                         item 1-2
00555 ------------------------------------------------------- 1767769
                                                         item 3
00557 ------------------------------------------------------- 1767769
                                                         item 4
00560-00561 ------------------------------------------------- 1767769
                                                         item 5-6
00563-00565 ------------------------------------------------- 1767769
                                                         item 7-9
00568-00571 ------------------------------------------------- 1767770
                                                         item 1-4
00574-00575 ------------------------------------------------- 1767770
                                                         item 5-6
```

```
00692  ------------------------------------------------- 1767391
                                                          item 9
00695-00696  ------------------------------------------- 1767391
                                                          item 10-11
00699  ------------------------------------------------- 1767391
                                                          item 12
00705-00706  ------------------------------------------- 1767391
                                                          item 13-14
00707-00712  ------------------------------------------- 1767392
                                                          item 1-6
00716-00719  ------------------------------------------- 1767392
                                                          item 7-10
00720-00726  ------------------------------------------- 1809135
                                                          item 1-6
00729  ------------------------------------------------- 1809135
                                                          item 7
00731  ------------------------------------------------- 1809135
                                                          item 8
00734-00737  ------------------------------------------- 1809135
                                                          item 9-12
00741  ------------------------------------------------- 1809135
                                                          item 13
00741  (cont.)  ----------------------------------------- 1809136
                                                          item 1
00742-00743  ------------------------------------------- 1809136
                                                          item 2-3
00745-00746  ------------------------------------------- 1809136
                                                          item 4-5
00748-00750  ------------------------------------------- 1809136
                                                          item 6-8
00753  ------------------------------------------------- 1809136
                                                          item 9
00757  ------------------------------------------------- 1809136
                                                          item 10
00762  ------------------------------------------------- 1809136
                                                          item 11
00766-00767  ------------------------------------------- 1809136
                                                          item 12-13
00774  ------------------------------------------------- 1809136
                                                          item 14
00776-00777  ------------------------------------------- 1809136
                                                          item 15-16
00781  ------------------------------------------------- 1809136
                                                          item 17
00783  ------------------------------------------------- 1809136
                                                          item 18
00784  ------------------------------------------------- 1809137
                                                          item 1
00787-00788  ------------------------------------------- 1809137
                                                          item 2-3
00794-00795  ------------------------------------------- 1809137
                                                          item 4-5
00798  ------------------------------------------------- 1809137
                                                          item 6
00799-00803  ------------------------------------------- 1809137
                                                          item 7-11
00807  ------------------------------------------------- 1809137
                                                          item 12
00810-00811  ------------------------------------------- 1809137
                                                          item 13-14
00819  ------------------------------------------------- 1809137
                                                          item 15
```

```
00825 -------------------------------------------------------- 1809137
                                                            item 16
00828-00829 -------------------------------------------------- 1809137
                                                          item 17-18
00830-00831 -------------------------------------------------- 1807409
                                                          item 11-13
00833 -------------------------------------------------------- 1807409
                                                            item 14
00835 -------------------------------------------------------- 1807409
                                                            item 15
00841 -------------------------------------------------------- 1807409
                                                            item 16
00846 -------------------------------------------------------- 1807409
                                                            item 17
00848 -------------------------------------------------------- 1807409
                                                            item 18
00851 -------------------------------------------------------- 1807409
                                                            item 19
00853 -------------------------------------------------------- 1807409
                                                            item 20
00860 -------------------------------------------------------- 1807409
                                                            item 22
00862 -------------------------------------------------------- 1807409
                                                            item 23
00868-00869 -------------------------------------------------- 1807409
                                                          item 24-25
00877 -------------------------------------------------------- 1807409
                                                            item 26
00884-00885 -------------------------------------------------- 1807409
                                                          item 27-28
00887 -------------------------------------------------------- 1807409
                                                            item 29
00890-00893 -------------------------------------------------- 1807409
                                                          item 30-33
00895 -------------------------------------------------------- 1807409
                                                            item 34
00896 -------------------------------------------------------- 1807411
                                                            item 1
00900-00903 -------------------------------------------------- 1807411
                                                           item 2-5
00908 -------------------------------------------------------- 1807411
                                                            item 6
00910-00912 -------------------------------------------------- 1807411
                                                           item 7-9
00914 -------------------------------------------------------- 1807411
                                                            item 10
00916 -------------------------------------------------------- 1807411
                                                            item 11
00918-00919 -------------------------------------------------- 1807411
                                                          item 12-13
00912-00923 -------------------------------------------------- 1807411
                                                          item 14-17
00926 -------------------------------------------------------- 1807411
                                                            item 18
00928-00929 -------------------------------------------------- 1807411
                                                          item 19-20
00932 -------------------------------------------------------- 1807411
                                                            item 21
00934 -------------------------------------------------------- 1807411
                                                          item 22-23
00936 -------------------------------------------------------- 1807411
                                                            item 24
```

```
00940-00942 ------------------------------------------------- 1807411
                                                        item 25-27
00947-00950 --------------------------------------------- 1807412
                                                          item 1-4
00953 --------------------------------------------------- 1807412
                                                            item 5
00957-00965 ----------------------------------------------- 1807412
                                                         item 6-15
00967-00972 ----------------------------------------------- 1807412
                                                        item 16-20
00972-00973 ----------------------------------------------- 1807413
                                                          item 1-2
00976 --------------------------------------------------- 1807413
                                                            item 3
00980 --------------------------------------------------- 1807413
                                                            item 4
00984-00985 ------------------------------------------------- 1807413
                                                          item 5-6
00987 --------------------------------------------------- 1807413
                                                            item 7
00989-00990 --------------------------------------------- 1767701
                                                        item 13-14
00994-01000 --------------------------------------------- 1767701
                                                        item 15-20
01002 --------------------------------------------------- 1767701
                                                           item 21
01006 --------------------------------------------------- 1767701
                                                           item 22
01007 --------------------------------------------------- 1767702
                                                            item 1
01009 --------------------------------------------------- 1767702
                                                            item 2
01011 a-g ----------------------------------------------- 1767702
                                                            item 3
01013-01015 --------------------------------------------- 1767702
                                                          item 4-6
01017-01021 --------------------------------------------- 1767702
                                                         item 7-11
01025 --------------------------------------------------- 1767702
                                                           item 12
01027 --------------------------------------------------- 1767702
                                                           item 13
01029-01031 --------------------------------------------- 1767702
                                                        item 14-16
01034-01037 ----------------------------------------------- 1767702
                                                        item 17-20
01039 ----------------------------------------------------- 1767702
                                                           item 21
01042-01043 --------------------------------------------- 1767702
                                                        item 22-23
01045 --------------------------------------------------- 1767702
                                                           item 24
01046 --------------------------------------------------- 1767703
                                                            item 1
01051 --------------------------------------------------- 1767703
                                                            item 2
01054-01055 --------------------------------------------- 1767703
                                                          item 3-4
01057-01058 --------------------------------------------- 1767703
                                                          item 5-6
01063 --------------------------------------------------- 1767703
                                                            item 7
```

```
01187 ------------------------------------------------------ 1809606
                                                            item 2
01191 ------------------------------------------------------ 1809606
                                                            item 3
01193 ------------------------------------------------------ 1809606
                                                            item 4
0198-01199 ------------------------------------------------- 1809606
                                                            item 5-6
01203 ------------------------------------------------------ 1809606
                                                            item 7
01212 ------------------------------------------------------ 1809606
                                                            item 8
01214 ------------------------------------------------------ 1809606
                                                            item 9
01218 ------------------------------------------------------ 1809606
                                                            item 10
01222-01224 ------------------------------------------------ 1809606
                                                            item 11-13
01226-01228 ------------------------------------------------ 1809606
                                                            item 14-16
01230 ------------------------------------------------------ 1809606
                                                            item 17
01236-01239 ------------------------------------------------ 1809607
                                                            item 1-4
01242 ------------------------------------------------------ 1809607
                                                            item 5
01244-01245 ------------------------------------------------ 1809607
                                                            item 6-7
01247 ------------------------------------------------------ 1809607
                                                            item 8
01249 ------------------------------------------------------ 1809607
                                                            item 9
01251-01252 ------------------------------------------------ 1809607
                                                            item 10-11
01255-01258 ------------------------------------------------ 1809607
                                                            item 12-15
01259-01260 ------------------------------------------------ 1809607
                                                            item 16
01261-01262 ------------------------------------------------ 1809607
                                                            item 17-18
01265-01266 ------------------------------------------------ 1809607
                                                            item 19-20
01267-01269 ------------------------------------------------ 1767776
                                                            item 1-3
01271-01274 ------------------------------------------------ 1767776
                                                            item 4-7
01283 ------------------------------------------------------ 1767776
                                                            item 8
01287-01288 ------------------------------------------------ 1767776
                                                            item 9-10
01292-01293 ------------------------------------------------ 1767776
                                                            item 11-12
01296 ------------------------------------------------------ 1767776
                                                            item 13
01298 ------------------------------------------------------ 1767776
                                                            item 14
01300-01301 ------------------------------------------------ 1767776
                                                            item 15-16
01304 ------------------------------------------------------ 1767776
                                                            item 17
01307 ------------------------------------------------------ 1767776
                                                            item 18
```

```
01310-01313 ----------------------------------------------- 1767776
                                                    item 19-22
01315-01316 ----------------------------------------------- 1767776
                                                    item 23-24
01318 ----------------------------------------------------- 1767777
                                                       item 1
01321 ----------------------------------------------------- 1767777
                                                       item 2
01324 ----------------------------------------------------- 1767777
                                                       item 3
01326 ----------------------------------------------------- 1767777
                                                       item 4
01328 ----------------------------------------------------- 1767777
                                                       item 5
01332 ----------------------------------------------------- 1767777
                                                       item 6
01334 ----------------------------------------------------- 1767777
                                                      item 7-8
01337-01338 ----------------------------------------------- 1767777
                                                     item 9-10
01340-01343 ----------------------------------------------- 1767777
                                                    item 11-14
01345-01346 ----------------------------------------------- 1767777
                                                    item 15-16
01348 ----------------------------------------------------- 1767777
                                                      item 17
01354-01357 ----------------------------------------------- 1767777
                                                    item 18-21
01359 ----------------------------------------------------- 1767777
                                                      item 22
01361 ----------------------------------------------------- 1767777
                                                      item 23
01362-01366 ----------------------------------------------- 1767778
                                                     item 1-5
01372 ----------------------------------------------------- 1767778
                                                       item 6
01375 ----------------------------------------------------- 1767392
                                                    item 11-12
01375-01377 ----------------------------------------------- 1767393
                                                     item 1-3
01380-01382 ----------------------------------------------- 1767393
                                                     item 4-6
01384 no. 2 ----------------------------------------------- 1767393
                                                       item 7
01386-01388 ----------------------------------------------- 1767393
                                                    item 8-10
01390 ----------------------------------------------------- 1767393
                                                      item 11
01392-01393 ----------------------------------------------- 1767393
                                                    item 12-13
01395-01400 ----------------------------------------------- 1767393
                                                    item 14-19
01402-01405 ----------------------------------------------- 1767393
                                                    item 20-24
01406-01408 ----------------------------------------------- 1767394
                                                     item 1-3
01411-01412 ----------------------------------------------- 1767394
                                                     item 4-5
01415 ----------------------------------------------------- 1767394
                                                       item 6
01418-01419 ----------------------------------------------- 1767394
                                                      item 7-8
```

```
01421 ---------------------------------------------------- 1767394
                                                         item 9
01423 ---------------------------------------------------- 1767394
                                                         item 10
01425-01426 ---------------------------------------------- 1767394
                                                        item 11-12
01428-01432 ---------------------------------------------- 1767394
                                                        item 13-14
01435 ---------------------------------------------------- 1767394
                                                         item 15
01437-01438 ---------------------------------------------- 1767394
                                                        item 16-17
01439 ---------------------------------------------------- 1809138
                                                         item 1
01441 ---------------------------------------------------- 1809138
                                                         item 2
01445 ---------------------------------------------------- 1809138
                                                         item 3
01450 ---------------------------------------------------- 1809138
                                                         item 4
01452-01453 ---------------------------------------------- 1809138
                                                        item 5-6
01455-01464 ---------------------------------------------- 1809138
                                                        item 7-16
01466 ---------------------------------------------------- 1809138
                                                         item 17
01469 ---------------------------------------------------- 1809138
                                                         item 18
01473 ---------------------------------------------------- 1809138
                                                         item 19
01475 ---------------------------------------------------- 1809138
                                                         item 20
01484 ---------------------------------------------------- 1809138
                                                         item 21
01486 ---------------------------------------------------- 1809139
                                                         item 1
01488 ---------------------------------------------------- 1809139
                                                         item 2
01490-01491 ---------------------------------------------- 1809139
                                                        item 3-4
01496 ---------------------------------------------------- 1809139
                                                         item 5
01498 ---------------------------------------------------- 1809139
                                                         item 6
01500 ---------------------------------------------------- 1809139
                                                         item 7
01506 ---------------------------------------------------- 1809139
                                                         item 8
01510 ---------------------------------------------------- 1809139
                                                         item 9
01514 ---------------------------------------------------- 1809139
                                                         item 10
01516 ---------------------------------------------------- 1809139
                                                         item 11
01518-01519 ---------------------------------------------- 1809139
                                                        item 12-13
01521 ---------------------------------------------------- 1809139
                                                         item 14
01523 ---------------------------------------------------- 1809139
                                                         item 15
01529-01532 ---------------------------------------------- 1809139
                                                        item 16-19
```

```
01535 ------------------------------------------------------- 1809139
                                                                item 20
01537 ------------------------------------------------------- 1809139
                                                                item 21
01539 ------------------------------------------------------- 1809139
                                                                item 22
01543-01546 ------------------------------------------------- 1809139
                                                              item 23-26
01549 ------------------------------------------------------- 1809139
                                                                item 27
01556-01557 ------------------------------------------------- 1809139
                                                              item 28-29
01560-01561 ------------------------------------------------- 1809139
                                                              item 30-31
01562-01566 ------------------------------------------------- 1809140
                                                               item 1-5
01568-01570 ------------------------------------------------- 1809140
                                                               item 6-8
01572 ------------------------------------------------------- 1809140
                                                                item 9
01578-01580 ------------------------------------------------- 1809140
                                                              item 10-12
01591 ------------------------------------------------------- 1809140
                                                                item 13
01593 ------------------------------------------------------- 1809140
                                                                item 14
01595 ------------------------------------------------------- 1809140
                                                                item 15
01599-01609 ------------------------------------------------- 1809140
                                                              item 16-19
01614 ------------------------------------------------------- 1809140
                                                                item 20
01616-01617 ------------------------------------------------- 1809140
                                                              item 21-22
01617   (cont.) --------------------------------------------- 1809141
                                                                item 1
01618 ------------------------------------------------------- 1809141
                                                               item 2-3
01620 ------------------------------------------------------- 1809141
                                                                item 4
01623-01626 ------------------------------------------------- 1809141
                                                               item 5-8
01628-01629 ------------------------------------------------- 1809141
                                                              item 9-10
01632 ------------------------------------------------------- 1809141
                                                                item 11
01634-01636 ------------------------------------------------- 1809157
                                                               item 6-8
01640 ------------------------------------------------------- 1809157
                                                                item 9
01641 ------------------------------------------------------- 1809158
                                                                item 1
01646 ------------------------------------------------------- 1809158
                                                                item 2
01648-01649 ------------------------------------------------- 1809158
                                                               item 3-4
01651 ------------------------------------------------------- 1809158
                                                                item 5
01653 ------------------------------------------------------- 1809158
                                                                item 6
01658-01659 ------------------------------------------------- 1809158
                                                               item 7-8
```

```
01661-01663 ------------------------------------------------ 1809158
                                                          item 9-11
01667 ------------------------------------------------------ 1809158
                                                          item 12
01669 ------------------------------------------------------ 1809158
                                                          item 13
01672 ------------------------------------------------------ 1809158
                                                          item 14
01974 ------------------------------------------------------ 1809159
                                                          item 1
01676-01678 ------------------------------------------------ 1809159
                                                          item 2-4
01680 ------------------------------------------------------ 1809159
                                                          item 5
01685-01687 ------------------------------------------------ 1809159
                                                          item 6-8
01689 ------------------------------------------------------ 1809159
                                                          item 9
01691-01692 ------------------------------------------------ 1809159
                                                          item 10-11
01698-01699 ------------------------------------------------ 1809159
                                                          item 12-13
01701 ------------------------------------------------------ 1809159
                                                          item 14
01703-01706 ------------------------------------------------ 1809159
                                                          item 15-18
01707-01709 ------------------------------------------------ 1809160
                                                          item 1-3
01712 ------------------------------------------------------ 1809160
                                                          item 4
01714-01718 ------------------------------------------------ 1809160
                                                          item 5-9
01722 ------------------------------------------------------ 1809160
                                                          item 10
01727-01728 ------------------------------------------------ 1809160
                                                          item 11-12
01730-01731 ------------------------------------------------ 1809160
                                                          item 13-14
01734 ------------------------------------------------------ 1809160
                                                          item 15
01736-01737 ------------------------------------------------ 1809160
                                                          item 16-17
01739 ------------------------------------------------------ 1809160
                                                          item 18
01744 ------------------------------------------------------ 1809182
                                                          item 1
01746 ------------------------------------------------------ 1767772
                                                          item 5
01761-01762 ------------------------------------------------ 1767772
                                                          item 6-7
01765 ------------------------------------------------------ 1767772
                                                          item 8
01768-01769 ------------------------------------------------ 1767772
                                                          item 9-10
01771 no. 1-4 ---------------------------------------------- 1767772
                                                          item 11-12
01776 ------------------------------------------------------ 1767772
                                                          item 13
01780 ------------------------------------------------------ 1767772
                                                          item 14
01783-01785 ------------------------------------------------ 1767772
                                                          item 15-17
```

```
01786-01792 ------------------------------------------------ 1767773
                                                            item 1-7
01794 ------------------------------------------------------ 1767773
                                                            item 8
01795 ------------------------------------------------------ 1767773
                                                            item 10
01798 ------------------------------------------------------ 1767773
                                                            item 9
01799 ------------------------------------------------------ 1767773
                                                            item 11
01801-01802 ------------------------------------------------ 1767773
                                                            item 12-13
01806-01810 ------------------------------------------------ 1767773
                                                            item 14-18
01812 ------------------------------------------------------ 1767773
                                                            item 19
01818-01821 ------------------------------------------------ 1767773
                                                            item 20-23
01825-01828 ------------------------------------------------ 1767773
                                                            item 24-27
01830 ------------------------------------------------------ 1767773
                                                            item 28
01836-01839 ------------------------------------------------ 1767773
                                                            item 29-32
01843 ------------------------------------------------------ 1767773
                                                            item 33
01850 ------------------------------------------------------ 1767773
                                                            item 34
01853-01854 ------------------------------------------------ 1767773
                                                            item 35-36
01856-01857 ------------------------------------------------ 1767773
                                                            item 37-38
01861 ------------------------------------------------------ 1767773
                                                            item 39
01864-01867 ------------------------------------------------ 1767754
                                                            item 1-5
01869-01871 ------------------------------------------------ 1807413
                                                            item 8-10
01873-01875 ------------------------------------------------ 1807413
                                                            item 11-13
01880-01881 ------------------------------------------------ 1807413
                                                            item 14-15
01884-01886 ------------------------------------------------ 1807413
                                                            item 16-18
01887-01893 ------------------------------------------------ 1807414
                                                            item 1-7
01896 ------------------------------------------------------ 1807414
                                                            item 8
01899-01901 ------------------------------------------------ 1807414
                                                            item 9-11
01903-01904 ------------------------------------------------ 1807414
                                                            item 12-13
01907 ------------------------------------------------------ 1807414
                                                            item 14
01909 ------------------------------------------------------ 1807414
                                                            item 15
01912 ------------------------------------------------------ 1807414
                                                            item 16
01916-01917 ------------------------------------------------ 1807414
                                                            item 17-18
01919 ------------------------------------------------------ 1807415
                                                            item 1
```

```
01923-01927 ------------------------------------------------ 1807415
                                                          item 2-7
01929-01930 ------------------------------------------------ 1807415
                                                          item 8-9
01932 ------------------------------------------------------ 1807415
                                                          item 10
01938 ------------------------------------------------------ 1807415
                                                          item 11
01941 ------------------------------------------------------ 1807415
                                                          item 12
01995 ------------------------------------------------------ 1807415
                                                          item 13
02000-02001 ------------------------------------------------ 1807415
                                                          item 14-15
02004 ------------------------------------------------------ 1807415
                                                          item 16
02008-02009 ------------------------------------------------ 1807415
                                                          item 17-18
02016-02017 ------------------------------------------------ 1807415
                                                          item 19-20
02019 ------------------------------------------------------ 1807415
                                                          item 21
02022-02024 ------------------------------------------------ 1807415
                                                          item 21
02026-02028 ------------------------------------------------ 1807415
                                                          item 22-25
02030-02032 ------------------------------------------------ 1767778
                                                          item 7-10
02037 ------------------------------------------------------ 1767778
                                                          item 11
02039 ------------------------------------------------------ 1767778
                                                          item 12
02043 ------------------------------------------------------ 1767779
                                                          item 1
02046-02052 ------------------------------------------------ 1767779
                                                          item 2-7
02054-02058 ------------------------------------------------ 1767779
                                                          item 8-12
02060-02061 ------------------------------------------------ 1767779
                                                          item 13-14
02066-02068 ------------------------------------------------ 1767779
                                                          item 15-17
02073 ------------------------------------------------------ 1767779
                                                          item 18
02075 ------------------------------------------------------ 1767779
                                                          item 19
02079-02080 ------------------------------------------------ 1767779
                                                          item 20-21
02084 ------------------------------------------------------ 1767779
                                                          item 22
02087 ------------------------------------------------------ 1767779
                                                          item 23
02089 ------------------------------------------------------ 1767779
                                                          item 24
02090-02092 ------------------------------------------------ 1767780
                                                          item 1-3
02094-02095 ------------------------------------------------ 1767780
                                                          item 4-5
02097-02098 ------------------------------------------------ 1767780
                                                          item 6-7
02100-02108 ------------------------------------------------ 1767780
                                                          item 8-16
```

```
02110 -------------------------------------------------- 1767780
                                                  item 17
02112-02113 -------------------------------------------- 1767780
                                                  item 18-19
02115-02123 -------------------------------------------- 1767780
                                                  item 20-28
02123-02124 -------------------------------------------- 1809607
                                                  item 21-22
02126-02134 -------------------------------------------- 1809607
                                                  item 23-31
02140 -------------------------------------------------- 1809607
                                                  item 32
02141-02142 -------------------------------------------- 1809608
                                                  item 1-2
02144 -------------------------------------------------- 1809608
                                                  item 3
02148-02149 -------------------------------------------- 1809608
                                                  item 4-5
02151-02152 -------------------------------------------- 1809608
                                                  item 6-7
02155-02156 -------------------------------------------- 1809608
                                                  item 8-9
02159-02164 -------------------------------------------- 1809608
                                                  item 10-15
02167-02168 -------------------------------------------- 1809608
                                                  item 16-17
02172-02175 -------------------------------------------- 1809608
                                                  item 18-21
02183-02184 -------------------------------------------- 1809609
                                                  item 1-2
02192-02196 -------------------------------------------- 1809609
                                                  item 3-7
02198 -------------------------------------------------- 1809609
                                                  item 8
02204 -------------------------------------------------- 1809609
                                                  item 9
02206-02207 -------------------------------------------- 1809609
                                                  item 10-11
02215-02216 -------------------------------------------- 1809609
                                                  item 12-13
02219 -------------------------------------------------- 1809609
                                                  item 14
02224 -------------------------------------------------- 1809609
                                                  item 15
02229-02230 -------------------------------------------- 1809609
                                                  item 16-17
02231 -------------------------------------------------- 1809695
                                                  item 1
02236-02237 -------------------------------------------- 1809695
                                                  item 2-3
02240 -------------------------------------------------- 1809695
                                                  item 4
02242-02244 -------------------------------------------- 1809695
                                                  item 5-7
02252-02253 -------------------------------------------- 1809695
                                                  item 8-9
02256 -------------------------------------------------- 1809695
                                                  item 10
02258 -------------------------------------------------- 1809695
                                                  item 11
02260 -------------------------------------------------- 1809695
                                                  item 12
```

```
02262 ------------------------------------------------ 1809695
                                                    item 13
02266 ------------------------------------------------ 1809695
                                                    item 14
02268-02270 ------------------------------------------ 1809695
                                                    item 15-17
02273-02274 ------------------------------------------ 1809695
                                                    item 18-19
02276-02277 ------------------------------------------ 1809695
                                                    item 20-21
02278 ------------------------------------------------ 1809182
                                                    item 2
02282 ------------------------------------------------ 1809182
                                                    item 3
02286 ------------------------------------------------ 1809182
                                                    item 4
02288 ------------------------------------------------ 1809182
                                                    item 5
02290-02291 ------------------------------------------ 1809182
                                                    item 6-7
02295-02298 ------------------------------------------ 1809182
                                                    item 8-11
02300-02303 ------------------------------------------ 1809182
                                                    item 12-15
02305 ------------------------------------------------ 1809182
                                                    item 16
02307 ------------------------------------------------ 1809182
                                                    item 17
02316 ------------------------------------------------ 1809182
                                                    item 18
02318-02321 ------------------------------------------ 1809182
                                                    item 19-22
02323-02325 ------------------------------------------ 1809182
                                                    item 23-26
02330-02331 ------------------------------------------ 1809182
                                                    item 27-28
02332-02337 ------------------------------------------ 1809182
                                                    item 29-34
02340 ------------------------------------------------ 1809182
                                                    item 35
02340 ------------------------------------------------ 1809183
02340 ------------------------------------------------ 1809184
                                                    item 1
02341-02342 ------------------------------------------ 1809184
                                                    item 2-3
02344 ------------------------------------------------ 1809184
                                                    item 4
02346-02347 ------------------------------------------ 1809184
                                                    item 5-6
02349 ------------------------------------------------ 1809184
                                                    item 7
02351-02355 ------------------------------------------ 1809184
                                                    item 8-12
02357 ------------------------------------------------ 1809184
                                                    item 13
02360-02361 ------------------------------------------ 1809184
                                                    item 14-15
02363-02364 ------------------------------------------ 1809184
                                                    item 16-17
02366-02370 ------------------------------------------ 1809184
                                                    item 18-23
```

```
02372 --------------------------------------------------------- 1809184
                                                          item 24
02374-02378 --------------------------------------------------- 1809184
                                                          item 25-29
02385-02389 --------------------------------------------------- 1809185
                                                          item 1-5
02391 ----------------------------------------------------------- 1809185
                                                          item 6
02393 ----------------------------------------------------------- 1809185
                                                          item 7
02395 ----------------------------------------------------------- 1809185
                                                          item 8
02397 ----------------------------------------------------------- 1807396
                                                          item 1
03299-02401 --------------------------------------------------- 1807396
                                                          item 2-4
02403-02405 --------------------------------------------------- 1807396
                                                          item 5-7
02407-02408 --------------------------------------------------- 1807396
                                                          item 8-10
02410 a-b - 2411 ----------------------------------------------- 1807396
                                                          item 11-13
02413 ----------------------------------------------------------- 1807396
                                                          item 14
02416 ----------------------------------------------------------- 1807396
                                                          item 15
02418 ----------------------------------------------------------- 1807396
                                                          item 16
02422 ----------------------------------------------------------- 1807396
                                                          item 17
02427 ----------------------------------------------------------- 1807396
                                                          item 18
02429-02430 --------------------------------------------------- 1807396
                                                          item 19-20
02432-2433 ----------------------------------------------------- 1807397
                                                          item 1-2
02438-02439 --------------------------------------------------- 1807397
                                                          item 3-4
02441-02445 --------------------------------------------------- 1807397
                                                          item 5-9
02447 ----------------------------------------------------------- 1807397
                                                          item 10
02449 ----------------------------------------------------------- 1807397
                                                          item 11
02454-02455 --------------------------------------------------- 1807397
                                                          item 12-13
02457-02458 --------------------------------------------------- 1807397
                                                          item 14-15
02459-02461 --------------------------------------------------- 1807398
                                                          item 1-3
02463-02464 --------------------------------------------------- 1807398
                                                          item 4-5
02468-02471 --------------------------------------------------- 1807398
                                                          item 6-9
02476-02477 --------------------------------------------------- 1807398
                                                          item 10-11
02484 ----------------------------------------------------------- 1807398
                                                          item 12
02486 ----------------------------------------------------------- 1807398
                                                          item 13
02487 ----------------------------------------------------------- 1809141
                                                          item 12
```

```
02489 --------------------------------------------------------- 1809141
                                                          item 13
02491-02499 --------------------------------------------------- 1809141
                                                          item 14-22
02501-02502 --------------------------------------------------- 1809141
                                                          item 23-24
02504-02505 --------------------------------------------------- 1809141
                                                          item 25-26
02506 --------------------------------------------------------- 1809057
                                                          item 1
02511 --------------------------------------------------------- 1809057
                                                          item 2
02513-02514 --------------------------------------------------- 1809057
                                                          item 3-4
02530 --------------------------------------------------------- 1809057
                                                          item 5
02533 --------------------------------------------------------- 1809057
                                                          item 6
02541-02542 --------------------------------------------------- 1809057
                                                          item 7-8
02546 --------------------------------------------------------- 1809057
                                                          item 9
02548-02549 --------------------------------------------------- 1809057
                                                          item 10-11
02555 --------------------------------------------------------- 1809057
                                                          item 12
02557 --------------------------------------------------------- 1809057
                                                          item 13
02559 --------------------------------------------------------- 1809057
                                                          item 14
02561 --------------------------------------------------------- 1809057
                                                          item 15
02562-02563 --------------------------------------------------- 1809058
                                                          item 1-2
02565-02566 --------------------------------------------------- 1809058
                                                          item 3-4
02598-02572 --------------------------------------------------- 1809058
                                                          item 5-9
02574-02575 --------------------------------------------------- 1809058
                                                          item 10-11
02578 --------------------------------------------------------- 1809058
                                                          item 12
02581 --------------------------------------------------------- 1809058
                                                          item 13
02587 --------------------------------------------------------- 1809058
                                                          item 14
02589 --------------------------------------------------------- 1809058
                                                          item 15
02591 --------------------------------------------------------- 1809058
                                                          item 16-17
02595 --------------------------------------------------------- 1809058
                                                          item 18
02597 --------------------------------------------------------- 1809058
                                                          item 19
02598-02603 --------------------------------------------------- 1809059
                                                          item 1-6
02606-02608 --------------------------------------------------- 1809059
                                                          item 7-9
02610-02611 --------------------------------------------------- 1809059
                                                          item 10-11
02613-02616 --------------------------------------------------- 1809059
                                                          item 12-14
```

```
02617 ----------------------------------------------------- 1767394
                                                         item 18
02622-02625 ----------------------------------------------- 1767394
                                                         item 19-22
02627 ----------------------------------------------------- 1767394
                                                         item 23
02631-02633 ----------------------------------------------- 1767394
                                                         item 24-26
02634 ----------------------------------------------------- 1767395
                                                         item 1
02638-02641 ----------------------------------------------- 1767395
                                                         item 2-5
02645-02648 ----------------------------------------------- 1767395
                                                         item 6-9
02654-02656 I-IV ------------------------------------------ 1767395
                                                         item 10-12
02656 I-IV  (cont.) --------------------------------------- 1767396
02656 I-IV  (cont.) --------------------------------------- 1767357
                                                         item 1
02657-02662 ----------------------------------------------- 1767754
                                                         item 6-10
02665-02666 ----------------------------------------------- 1767754
                                                         item 11-12
02676-02680 ----------------------------------------------- 1767754
                                                         item 13-17
02682-02685 ----------------------------------------------- 1767754
                                                         item 18-21
02687-02688 ----------------------------------------------- 1767755
                                                         item 1-2
02690 ----------------------------------------------------- 1767755
                                                         item 3
02693-02695 ----------------------------------------------- 1767755
                                                         item 4-6
02697 ----------------------------------------------------- 1767755
                                                         item 7
02699 ----------------------------------------------------- 1767755
                                                         item 8
02707-02712 ----------------------------------------------- 1767755
                                                         item 9-15
02721-02723 ----------------------------------------------- 1767755
                                                         item 16-18
02726 ----------------------------------------------------- 1767756
                                                         item 1
02728 ----------------------------------------------------- 1767756
                                                         item 2
02730 ----------------------------------------------------- 1767756
                                                         item 3
02739-02742 ----------------------------------------------- 1767756
                                                         item 4-9
02743-02749 ----------------------------------------------- 1767704
                                                         item 1-7
02754 ----------------------------------------------------- 1767704
                                                         item 8
02758-02759 ----------------------------------------------- 1767704
                                                         item 9-10
02816-02819 ----------------------------------------------- 1767704
                                                         item 11-14
02821-02824 ----------------------------------------------- 1767704
                                                         item 15-18
02825-02826 ----------------------------------------------- 1767705
                                                         item 1-2
```

```
02828-02829 ------------------------------------------------- 1767705
                                                        item 3-4
02831 ------------------------------------------------------- 1767705
                                                        item 5
02833-02835 ------------------------------------------------- 1767705
                                                        item 6-8
02837 ------------------------------------------------------- 1767705
                                                        item 9
02847-02854 ------------------------------------------------- 1767705
                                                        item 10-17
02855-02856 ------------------------------------------------- 1767706
                                                        item 1-2
02858-02859 ------------------------------------------------- 1767706
                                                        item 3-4
02862 ------------------------------------------------------- 1767706
                                                        item 5
02864 ------------------------------------------------------- 1767706
                                                        item 6
02866-02875 ------------------------------------------------- 1767706
                                                        item 7-16
02893-02894 ------------------------------------------------- 1767706
                                                        item 17-18
02897-02905 ------------------------------------------------- 1767706
                                                        item 19-27
02908-02909 ------------------------------------------------- 1767706
                                                        item 28-29
02910 ------------------------------------------------------- 1767689
                                                        item 1
02911-02916 ------------------------------------------------- 1767357
                                                        item 2-14
02918-02919 ------------------------------------------------- 1767357
                                                        item 15-16
02921-02922 ------------------------------------------------- 1767357
                                                        item 17-18
02925-02929 ------------------------------------------------- 1767357
                                                        item 19-22
02931 ------------------------------------------------------- 1767357
                                                        item 23
02934-02936 ------------------------------------------------- 1767357
                                                        item 24-26
02939 ------------------------------------------------------- 1767357
                                                        item 27
02947-02948 ------------------------------------------------- 1767357
                                                        item 28-29
02950-02951 ------------------------------------------------- 1767357
                                                        item 30-31
02953-02954 ------------------------------------------------- 1767358
                                                        item 1-2
02956 ------------------------------------------------------- 1767358
                                                        item 3
02958-02959 ------------------------------------------------- 1767358
                                                        item 4-5
02962 ------------------------------------------------------- 1767358
                                                        item 6
02964 ------------------------------------------------------- 1767358
                                                        item 7
02967-02969 ------------------------------------------------- 1767358
                                                        item 8-10
02973-02974 ------------------------------------------------- 1767358
                                                        item 11-12
02976-02980 ------------------------------------------------- 1767358
                                                        item 13-17
```

```
03139-03140 ------------------------------------------------------ 1807400
                                                               item 1-2
03142 ------------------------------------------------------------ 1807400
                                                               item 3
03148 ------------------------------------------------------------ 1807400
                                                               item 4
03167 a ---------------------------------------------------------- 1807400
                                                               item 5
03199 ------------------------------------------------------------ 1807400
                                                               item 6
03521 ------------------------------------------------------------ 1807400
                                                               item 7
03523-03524 ------------------------------------------------------ 1807400
                                                               item 8-9
03526 ------------------------------------------------------------ 1807400
                                                               item 10
02573 ------------------------------------------------------------ 1807400
                                                               item 11
03532-03533 ------------------------------------------------------ 1807401
                                                               item 1
03535 ------------------------------------------------------------ 1807401
                                                               item 3
03537 ------------------------------------------------------------ 1809185
                                                               item 9
03541 ------------------------------------------------------------ 1809185
                                                               item 10
03555 ------------------------------------------------------------ 1809185
                                                               item 11
03561 ------------------------------------------------------------ 1809186
                                                               item 1
03580-03581 ------------------------------------------------------ 1809186
                                                               item 2-3
03584 ------------------------------------------------------------ 1809186
                                                               item 4
03891-03592 ------------------------------------------------------ 1809186
                                                               item 5-6
03594 ------------------------------------------------------------ 1809186
                                                               item 7
03600-03601 ------------------------------------------------------ 1809186
                                                               item 8-9
03604-03605 ------------------------------------------------------ 1809186
                                                               item 10-11
03611 ------------------------------------------------------------ 1809186
                                                               item 12
03625-03626 ------------------------------------------------------ 1809186
                                                               item 13-14
03629 ------------------------------------------------------------ 1809186
                                                               item 15
03631 ------------------------------------------------------------ 1809186
                                                               item 16
03635 ------------------------------------------------------------ 1809186
                                                               item 17
03639 ------------------------------------------------------------ 1809186
                                                               item 18
03648-03651 ------------------------------------------------------ 1809187
                                                               item 1-4
03653 ------------------------------------------------------------ 1809187
                                                               item 5
03655 ------------------------------------------------------------ 1809187
                                                               item 6-7
03659 ------------------------------------------------------------ 1809187
                                                               item 8
```

```
03669  ---------------------------------------------------------  1809187
                                                                 item 9
03675  ---------------------------------------------------------  1809187
                                                                 item 10
03978-03679  ---------------------------------------------------  1809187
                                                                 item 11-12
03985-03687  ---------------------------------------------------  1809187
                                                                 item 13-14
03693  ---------------------------------------------------------  1809187
                                                                 item 15
03702-03703  ---------------------------------------------------  1809187
                                                                 item 16-17
03713-03714  ---------------------------------------------------  1809187
                                                                 item 18-19
03721  ---------------------------------------------------------  1809187
                                                                 item 20
03726  ---------------------------------------------------------  1809187
                                                                 item 21
03732  ---------------------------------------------------------  1809187
                                                                 item 22
03736  ---------------------------------------------------------  1809187
                                                                 item 23
03738  ---------------------------------------------------------  1809187
                                                                 item 24
03808-03809  ---------------------------------------------------  1809187
                                                                 item 25-26
03811  ---------------------------------------------------------  1809187
                                                                 item 27
03837  ---------------------------------------------------------  1809187
                                                                 item 28
03842  ---------------------------------------------------------  1809187
                                                                 item 29
03845  ---------------------------------------------------------  1809187
                                                                 item 30
03876  ---------------------------------------------------------  1809187
                                                                 item 31
03881  ---------------------------------------------------------  1767780
                                                                 item 29
03884  ---------------------------------------------------------  1767780
                                                                 item 30
03891  ---------------------------------------------------------  1767780
                                                                 item 31
03898-03899  ---------------------------------------------------  1767784
                                                                 item 1-2
03912-03913  ---------------------------------------------------  1767784
                                                                 item 3-4
03915-03917  ---------------------------------------------------  1767784
                                                                 item 5-6
03921  ---------------------------------------------------------  1767784
                                                                 item 7
03924-03926  ---------------------------------------------------  1767784
                                                                 item 8-10
03934-03935  ---------------------------------------------------  1767784
                                                                 item 11-12
03942-03945  ---------------------------------------------------  1767784
                                                                 item 13-16
03947  ---------------------------------------------------------  1767784
                                                                 item 17
03856  ---------------------------------------------------------  1767784
                                                                 item 18
03859-03963  ---------------------------------------------------  1767784
                                                                 item 19-23
```

```
04454 ----------------------------------------------- 1767759
                                              item 16
04456-04460 ------------------------------------------ 1767759
                                              item 17-21
04465 ----------------------------------------------- 1767759
                                              item 22
04469 ----------------------------------------------- 1767759
                                              item 23
04472-04473 ------------------------------------------ 1767759
                                              item 24-25
04476-04477 ------------------------------------------ 1767759
                                              item 26-27
04490 ----------------------------------------------- 1767689
                                              item 2
04494-04495 ------------------------------------------ 1767689
                                              item 3-4
04498-04499 ------------------------------------------ 1767689
                                              item 5-6
04501 ----------------------------------------------- 1767689
                                              item 7
04503 ----------------------------------------------- 1767689
                                              item 8
04505 ----------------------------------------------- 1767689
                                              item 9
04514-04515 ------------------------------------------ 1767689
                                              item 9
04517 ----------------------------------------------- 1767689
                                              item 12
04533-04534 ------------------------------------------ 1767689
                                              item 13-14
04535-04536 ------------------------------------------ 1767690
                                              item 1-2
04538 ----------------------------------------------- 1767690
                                              item 3
04542-04543 ------------------------------------------ 1767690
                                              item 4-5
04546 ----------------------------------------------- 1767690
                                              item 6
04550 ----------------------------------------------- 1767690
                                              item 7
04552-04553 ------------------------------------------ 1767690
                                              item 8-9
04557 ----------------------------------------------- 1767690
                                              item 10
04566 ----------------------------------------------- 1767690
                                              item 11
04568 ----------------------------------------------- 1767690
                                              item 12
04571-04572 ------------------------------------------ 1767690
                                              item 13-14
04579-04581 ------------------------------------------ 1767690
                                              item 15-17
04583 ----------------------------------------------- 1767690
                                              item 18
04585-04590 ------------------------------------------ 1767690
                                              item 19-24
04591 ----------------------------------------------- 1767691
                                              item 1
04596 ----------------------------------------------- 1767691
                                              item 2
04605-04606 ------------------------------------------ 1767691
                                              item 3-4
```

```
04616-04619 ------------------------------------------------ 1767691
                                                         item 5-8
04627 ------------------------------------------------------ 1767691
                                                         item 9
04633-04634 ------------------------------------------------ 1767691
                                                         item 10-11
04647-04648 ------------------------------------------------ 1767691
                                                         item 12-13
04651 ------------------------------------------------------ 1767691
                                                         item 14
04657 ------------------------------------------------------ 1767691
                                                         item 15
04659 ------------------------------------------------------ 1767691
                                                         item 16
04662 ------------------------------------------------------ 1767691
                                                         item 17
04663 ------------------------------------------------------ 1767692
                                                         item 1
04668 ------------------------------------------------------ 1809696
                                                         item 1
04670-04671 ------------------------------------------------ 1809696
                                                         item 2-3
04673 ------------------------------------------------------ 1809696
                                                         item 4
04679 ------------------------------------------------------ 1809696
                                                         item 5
04681 ------------------------------------------------------ 1809696
                                                         item 6
04689 ------------------------------------------------------ 1809696
                                                         item 7
04706 ------------------------------------------------------ 1809697
                                                         item 1
04717-04719 ------------------------------------------------ 1809697
                                                         item 2-4
04722 ------------------------------------------------------ 1809697
                                                         item 5
04726 ------------------------------------------------------ 1809697
                                                         item 6
04742 ------------------------------------------------------ 1809697
                                                         item 7
04743-04746 ------------------------------------------------ 1767359
                                                         item 14-17
04756 ------------------------------------------------------ 1767359
                                                         item 18
04765 ------------------------------------------------------ 1767359
                                                         item 19
04770 no. 1-2 --------------------------------------------- 1767359
                                                         item 20
04772-04773 ------------------------------------------------ 1767359
                                                         item 21-22
04777 ------------------------------------------------------ 1767359
                                                         item 23
04781 ------------------------------------------------------ 1767359
                                                         item 24
04784 no. 1-2 --------------------------------------------- 1767360
                                                         item 1
04791-04792 no. 3 ----------------------------------------- 1767360
                                                         item 2-3
04795 ------------------------------------------------------ 1767360
                                                         item 4
04800 ------------------------------------------------------ 1767360
                                                         item 5
```

```
04808 --------------------------------------------------- 1767360
                                                            item 6
04815-04816 ------------------------------------------- 1767360
                                                          item 7-8
04820 --------------------------------------------------- 1767360
                                                            item 9
04827 --------------------------------------------------- 1767360
                                                          item 10-11
04840-04841 ------------------------------------------- 1767360
                                                          item 12-13
04850-04851 ------------------------------------------- 1767360
                                                          item 14-15
04861 --------------------------------------------------- 1767360
                                                           item 16
04866 --------------------------------------------------- 1767361
                                                            item 1
04866 --------------------------------------------------- 1767360
                                                           item 17
04871 --------------------------------------------------- 1767361
                                                            item 2
04873 --------------------------------------------------- 1767361
                                                            item 3
04877-04878 ------------------------------------------- 1767361
                                                          item 4-5
04881 --------------------------------------------------- 1767361
                                                            item 6
04885 --------------------------------------------------- 1767361
                                                            item 7
04888 --------------------------------------------------- 1767361
                                                          item 8-9
04893 --------------------------------------------------- 1767361
                                                           item 10
04900 --------------------------------------------------- 1767361
                                                           item 11
04905 --------------------------------------------------- 1767361
                                                           item 12
04907 --------------------------------------------------- 1767361
                                                           item 13
04915 --------------------------------------------------- 1767361
                                                           item 14
04922 --------------------------------------------------- 1767361
                                                           item 15
04924 --------------------------------------------------- 1807401
                                                            item 4
04928 --------------------------------------------------- 1807401
                                                            item 5
04930 --------------------------------------------------- 1807401
                                                            item 6
04932-04933 ------------------------------------------- 1807401
                                                          item 7-8
04936 --------------------------------------------------- 1807401
                                                            item 9
04938-04939 ------------------------------------------- 1807401
                                                          item 10-11
04939 --------------------------------------------------- 1807402
                                                            item 1
04942 --------------------------------------------------- 1807402
                                                            item 2
04943 --------------------------------------------------- 1807402
                                                           item 14
04945 --------------------------------------------------- 1807402
                                                            item 3
```

```
04948 ------------------------------------------------ 1807402
                                                      item 4
04950-04951 --------------------------------------- 1807402
                                                    item 5-6
04953 ------------------------------------------------ 1807402
                                                      item 7
04960 ------------------------------------------------ 1807402
                                                      item 8
04970 ------------------------------------------------ 1807402
                                                      item 9
04973 ------------------------------------------------ 1807402
                                                   item 10-11
04977 ------------------------------------------------ 1807402
                                                   item 12-13
04992 ------------------------------------------------ 1807402
                                                     item 15
05006 ------------------------------------------------ 1807403
                                                      item 1
05007 ------------------------------------------------ 1809188
                                                      item 1
05011-05012 --------------------------------------- 1809188
                                                    item 2-3
05016 ------------------------------------------------ 1809188
                                                      item 4
05029-05030 --------------------------------------- 1809188
                                                    item 5-6
05033 ------------------------------------------------ 1809188
                                                      item 7
05034 ------------------------------------------------ 1807402
                                                     item 11
05035 ------------------------------------------------ 1809188
                                                      item 8
05046-05047 --------------------------------------- 1809188
                                                    item 9-10
05050-05051 --------------------------------------- 1809188
                                                   item 11-12
05053 ------------------------------------------------ 1809188
                                                     item 13
05061-05062 --------------------------------------- 1809188
                                                   item 14-15
05064 ------------------------------------------------ 1809188
                                                   item 16-17
05066 ------------------------------------------------ 1809189
                                                      item 1
05069 ------------------------------------------------ 1809189
                                                      item 2
05076-05077 --------------------------------------- 1809189
                                                    item 3-4
05081-05082 --------------------------------------- 1809189
                                                    item 5-6
05085-05086 --------------------------------------- 1809189
                                                    item 7-8
05090 ------------------------------------------------ 1809189
                                                      item 9
05094 ------------------------------------------------ 1809189
                                                     item 10
05098 ------------------------------------------------ 1809189
                                                     item 11
05113 ------------------------------------------------ 1809189
                                                     item 12
05116 ------------------------------------------------ 1809189
                                                     item 13
```

```
05119 ------------------------------------------------ 1809189
                                                       item 14
05122-05123 ---------------------------------------- 1809189
                                                      item 15-16
05127 a -------------------------------------------- 1809190
                                                       item 1
05130 ------------------------------------------------ 1809190
                                                       item 2
05132 ------------------------------------------------ 1809190
                                                       item 3
05137-05140 ---------------------------------------- 1809190
                                                      item 4-7
05147-05149 ---------------------------------------- 1809190
                                                     item 8-10
05151-05153 ---------------------------------------- 1809190
                                                    item 11-13
05147 ------------------------------------------------ 1809190
                                                       item 14
05159 ------------------------------------------------ 1809190
                                                       item 15
05163 ------------------------------------------------ 1809190
                                                       item 16
05165 ------------------------------------------------ 1809190
                                                       item 17
05168-05171 ---------------------------------------- 1809190
                                                    item 18-21
05179 ------------------------------------------------ 1809190
                                                       item 22
05185 ------------------------------------------------ 1809190
                                                       item 23
05187 ------------------------------------------------ 1809190
                                                       item 24
05193 ------------------------------------------------ 1809190
                                                       item 25
05198 ------------------------------------------------ 1809190
                                                    item 26-27
05203 ------------------------------------------------ 1767779
                                                       item 12
05204 ------------------------------------------------ 1809190
                                                       item 28
05209 ------------------------------------------------ 1809191
                                                       item 1
05212 ------------------------------------------------ 1809191
                                                       item 2
05213 ------------------------------------------------ 1809062
                                                       item 8
05215-05217 ---------------------------------------- 1809062
                                                     item 9-11
05220 ------------------------------------------------ 1809062
                                                       item 12
05225 ------------------------------------------------ 1809062
                                                       item 13
05232 ------------------------------------------------ 1809062
                                                       item 14
05240 ------------------------------------------------ 1809062
                                                       item 15
05243-05244 ---------------------------------------- 1809062
                                                    item 16-17
05246-05247 ---------------------------------------- 1809062
                                                    item 18-19
05248 ------------------------------------------------ 1809063
                                                       item 1
```

```
05256-05258 ----------------------------------------------- 1809063
                                                                item 2
05262 ----------------------------------------------------- 1809063
                                                                item 3
05265 ----------------------------------------------------- 1809063
                                                              item 4-5
05274 ----------------------------------------------------- 1809063
                                                                item 6
05276-05278 ----------------------------------------------- 1809063
                                                              item 7-9
05289-05290 ----------------------------------------------- 1809063
                                                            item 10-11
05295 ----------------------------------------------------- 1809063
                                                               item 12
05297 ----------------------------------------------------- 1809063
                                                               item 13
05302 ----------------------------------------------------- 1809063
                                                               item 14
05306-05307 ----------------------------------------------- 1809063
                                                            item 15-16
05309 ----------------------------------------------------- 1809063
                                                               item 17
05314 ----------------------------------------------------- 1809063
                                                               item 18
05314   (cont.) ------------------------------------------- 1809064
                                                                item 1
05319 ----------------------------------------------------- 1809064
                                                                item 2
05329 ----------------------------------------------------- 1809064
                                                                item 3
05332 ----------------------------------------------------- 1809064
                                                                item 4
05346 ----------------------------------------------------- 1809064
                                                                item 5
05359 ----------------------------------------------------- 1809064
                                                                item 6
05363 ----------------------------------------------------- 1809064
                                                                item 7
05367 ----------------------------------------------------- 1809064
                                                                item 8
05369-05370 ----------------------------------------------- 1809064
                                                              item 9-10
05372 ----------------------------------------------------- 1809064
                                                               item 11
05382 ----------------------------------------------------- 1809064
                                                               item 12
05384 ----------------------------------------------------- 1809064
                                                               item 13
05389 ----------------------------------------------------- 1809064
                                                               item 14
05406 ----------------------------------------------------- 1809064
                                                               item 15
05410 ----------------------------------------------------- 1809064
                                                               item 16
05415 ----------------------------------------------------- 1809065
                                                                item 1
05423 ----------------------------------------------------- 1809065
                                                                item 2
05455 ----------------------------------------------------- 1809065
                                                                item 3
05463 ----------------------------------------------------- 1767786
                                                                item 1
```

```
05664  (cont.) --------------------------------------- 1767760
                                                  item 1-2
05668 ------------------------------------------------ 1767760
                                                  item 3
05668  (cont.) --------------------------------------- 1767761
                                                  item 1
05674 ------------------------------------------------ 1767761
                                                  item 2
05676 ------------------------------------------------ 1767761
                                                  item 3
05691 ------------------------------------------------ 1767761
                                                  item 4
05693 ------------------------------------------------ 1767761
                                                  item 5
05699 ------------------------------------------------ 1767761
                                                  item 7
05710-05711 -------------------------------------------- 1767761
                                                  item 8-9
05716 ------------------------------------------------ 1767761
                                                  item 10
05723-05726 -------------------------------------------- 1767761
                                                  item 11-14
05729 ------------------------------------------------ 1767761
                                                  item 15
05734 ------------------------------------------------ 1807574
                                                  item 1
05737-05738 -------------------------------------------- 1807574
                                                  item 2-3
05745-05746 -------------------------------------------- 1807574
                                                  item 4-5
05752 ------------------------------------------------ 1807574
                                                  item 6
05759-05760 -------------------------------------------- 1807574
                                                  item 7-8
05762 ------------------------------------------------ 1807574
                                                  item 9
05764-05765 -------------------------------------------- 1807574
                                                  item 10-11
05770 ------------------------------------------------ 1807403
                                                  item 2
05772 ------------------------------------------------ 1807403
                                                  item 3
05786-05787 a ------------------------------------------ 1807403
                                                  item 4-5
05787  b ---------------------------------------------- 1807404
05787  c ---------------------------------------------- 1807475
05787  d ---------------------------------------------- 1807476
05787  e ---------------------------------------------- 1807477
05787  f ---------------------------------------------- 1807478
05787  g ---------------------------------------------- 1807479
05787  h ---------------------------------------------- 1807480
05787  i ---------------------------------------------- 1807481
                                                  item 1
05788-05790 -------------------------------------------- 1809697
                                                  item 8-10
05790  (cont.) --------------------------------------- 1809698
                                                  item 1
05791-05792 -------------------------------------------- 1809698
                                                  item 2-3
05076 ------------------------------------------------ 1809698
                                                  item 4
```

```
05803-05804 ------------------------------------------------- 1809698
                                                        item 5
05809-05810 ------------------------------------------------- 1809699
                                                        item 1-2
05811 ------------------------------------------------------- 1809698
                                                        item 5
05815 ------------------------------------------------------- 1809699
                                                        item 3
05820 ------------------------------------------------------- 1809699
                                                        item 4
05823 ------------------------------------------------------- 1809699
                                                        item 5
05826 ------------------------------------------------------- 1809698
                                                        item 5
05827 ------------------------------------------------------- 1767761
                                                        item 3
05829-05830 ------------------------------------------------- 1809699
                                                        item 6-7
05833 ------------------------------------------------------- 1809699
                                                        item 8
05846 ------------------------------------------------------- 1809698
                                                        item 5
05854-05855 ------------------------------------------------- 1809699
                                                        item 9-10
05861 ------------------------------------------------------- 1809699
                                                        item 11
05875 ------------------------------------------------------- 1809699
                                                        item 12
05881 ------------------------------------------------------- 1809698
                                                        item 5
05882 ------------------------------------------------------- 1767692
                                                        item 2
05886 ------------------------------------------------------- 1767692
                                                        item 3
05892 ------------------------------------------------------- 1767692
                                                        item 4
05894 ------------------------------------------------------- 1767692
                                                        item 5
05908-05909 ------------------------------------------------- 1809698
                                                        item 5
05911 ------------------------------------------------------- 1767692
                                                        item 6
05912 ------------------------------------------------------- 1767693
                                                        item 1-2
05927 ------------------------------------------------------- 1767693
                                                        item 3
05932 ------------------------------------------------------- 1767693
                                                        item 4
05935 ------------------------------------------------------- 1767693
                                                        item 5
05938 ------------------------------------------------------- 1767693
                                                        item 6
05943 ------------------------------------------------------- 1809698
                                                        item 5
05971-05972 ------------------------------------------------- 1809698
                                                        item 5
05975 ------------------------------------------------------- 1767693
                                                        item 8
05981 ------------------------------------------------------- 1767693
                                                        item 8
05991 ------------------------------------------------------- 1767693
                                                        item 9
```

```
05996 ------------------------------------------------- 1767694
                                                           item 1
05999 ------------------------------------------------- 1767698
                                                           item 5
06006 ------------------------------------------------- 1767694
                                                           item 2
06009 ------------------------------------------------- 1767694
                                                           item 3
06002 ------------------------------------------------- 1767694
                                                           item 5
06029 ------------------------------------------------- 1767694
                                                           item 4
06045 ------------------------------------------------- 1767694
                                                           item 6
06053-06055 ------------------------------------------- 1809698
                                                           item 5
06064 ------------------------------------------------- 1767694
                                                           item 7
06065-06066 ------------------------------------------- 1809698
                                                           item 5
06067 ------------------------------------------------- 1767694
                                                           item 8
06070 a ----------------------------------------------- 1767694
                                                           item 9
06073 ------------------------------------------------- 1809698
                                                           item 5
06080 ------------------------------------------------- 1767694
                                                           item 10
06082 ------------------------------------------------- 1767694
                                                           item 11
06091 ------------------------------------------------- 1767694
                                                           item 12
06093-06097 ------------------------------------------- 1809698
                                                           item 5
06107 ------------------------------------------------- 1809191
                                                           item 3
06111 ------------------------------------------------- 1809698
                                                           item 5
06112-06113 ------------------------------------------- 1809191
                                                           item 4-5
06121-06122 ------------------------------------------- 1809191
                                                           item 6-7
06130 ------------------------------------------------- 1809191
                                                           item 8
06144 ------------------------------------------------- 1809191
                                                           item 9
06151 ------------------------------------------------- 1809191
                                                           item 10
06158-06160 ------------------------------------------- 1809698
                                                           item 5
06161 ------------------------------------------------- 1809191
                                                           item 11
06164 ------------------------------------------------- 1809191
                                                           item 12
06170 ------------------------------------------------- 1809191
                                                           item 13
06180-06181 ------------------------------------------- 1809191
                                                           item 14-15
06186-06187 ------------------------------------------- 1809698
                                                           item 5
06191 ------------------------------------------------- 1809191
                                                           item 16
```

```
07194 ------------------------------------------------- 1807578
                                                      item 10
07196-07201 ------------------------------------------ 1807579
                                                     item 1-6
07203-07208 ------------------------------------------ 1807579
                                                     item 7-9
07205 ------------------------------------------------- 1807580
                                                      item 1
07209-07210 ------------------------------------------ 1807580
                                                     item 2-3
07211-07213 ------------------------------------------ 1809193
                                                   item 17-19
07215 ------------------------------------------------- 1809193
                                                     item 20
07217 ------------------------------------------------- 1809193
                                                     item 21
07219 ------------------------------------------------- 1809193
                                                     item 22
07219-07221 ------------------------------------------ 1809194
                                                     item 1-3
07223-07225 ------------------------------------------ 1807579
                                                      item 9
07226-07229 ------------------------------------------ 1809194
                                                     item 4-7
07229-07232 ------------------------------------------ 1809195
                                                     item 1-4
07234 ------------------------------------------------- 1807579
                                                      item 9
07235 ------------------------------------------------- 1809195
                                                      item 5
07236-07237 ------------------------------------------ 1807579
                                                      item 9
07238-07242 ------------------------------------------ 1809195
                                                    item 6-10
07243 ------------------------------------------------- 1807579
                                                      item 9
07244-07250 ------------------------------------------ 1809195
                                                   item 11-17
07251-07253 ------------------------------------------ 1809196
                                                     item 1-3
07254 ------------------------------------------------- 1807579
                                                      item 9
07255-07257 ------------------------------------------ 1809196
                                                     item 4-6
07259-07263 ------------------------------------------ 1809196
                                                    item 7-11
07264 ------------------------------------------------- 1807579
                                                      item 9
07266-07268 ------------------------------------------ 1767790
                                                     item 5-7
07269-07273 ------------------------------------------ 1767791
                                                     item 1-5
07275 ------------------------------------------------- 1807579
                                                      item 9
07276-07279 ------------------------------------------ 1767791
                                                     item 6-9
07280-07285 ------------------------------------------ 1767792
07286-07287 ------------------------------------------ 1767697
                                                     item 4-5
07289-07290 ------------------------------------------ 1767697
                                                     item 6-7
```

```
07290-07301 ------------------------------------------------- 1767698
07303-07310 ------------------------------------------------- 1767556
07311-07314 ------------------------------------------------- 1767557
                                                            item 1-4
07315-07323 ------------------------------------------------- 1809047
                                                            item 8-16
07324-0733 -------------------------------------------------- 1809048
07336-07341 ------------------------------------------------- 1809049
                                                            item 1-6
07343 ------------------------------------------------------- 1809049
                                                              item 7
07344 ------------------------------------------------------- 1809050
                                                              item 1
07346-07352 ------------------------------------------------- 1809702
                                                            item 5-11
07354-07356 ------------------------------------------------- 1809702
                                                           item 12-14
07357-07370 ------------------------------------------------- 1809703
07370  (cont.) --------------------------------------------- 1809723
                                                              item 1
07371-07374 ------------------------------------------------- 1809723
                                                            item 2-5
07374  (cont.) --------------------------------------------- 1809724
                                                              item 1
07375-07388 ------------------------------------------------- 1807580
                                                           item 4-17
07389-07397 ------------------------------------------------- 1807581
                                                           item 1-10
07399 ------------------------------------------------------- 1807581
                                                             item 11
07400 ------------------------------------------------------- 1807575
                                                              item 7
07401 ------------------------------------------------------- 1807581
                                                             item 12
07402-07407 ------------------------------------------------- 1807582
07408 1-2 b ------------------------------------------------- 1767365
07408 1-2 a ------------------------------------------------- 1767364
                                                             item 22
07408 c-07409 ----------------------------------------------- 1807560
07410-07414 ------------------------------------------------- 1807561
                                                            item 1-5
07416-07423 ------------------------------------------------- 1807481
                                                            item 2-9
07424-07427 ------------------------------------------------- 1807482
                                                            item 1-5
07429-07440 ------------------------------------------------- 1807482
                                                           item 6-12
07442 ------------------------------------------------------- 1807482
                                                             item 13
07443-07450 ------------------------------------------------- 1807483
                                                            item 1-8
07451-07454 ------------------------------------------------- 1809196
                                                           item 12-17
07454  (cont.) --------------------------------------------- 1809197
                                                              item 1
07457-07458 ------------------------------------------------- 1809197
                                                            item 2-3
07459 ------------------------------------------------------- 1809197
                                                              item 4
07460 ------------------------------------------------------- 1809197
                                                              item 3
```

```
07461-07470 ---------------------------------------------- 1809197
                                                        item 5-14
   07470  (cont.) --------------------------------------- 1809198
                                                          item 1
   07471-07484 ---------------------------------------------- 1809198
                                                       item 2-15
   07485-07488 ---------------------------------------------- 1807485
                                                        item 1-4
   07490-07496 ---------------------------------------------- 1807485
                                                       item 5-11
   07497-07514 ---------------------------------------------- 1807486
   07514 --------------------------------------------------- 1807561
                                                          item 6
   07515-07524 ---------------------------------------------- 1807487
   07525-07527 ---------------------------------------------- 1807583
   07527-07529 ---------------------------------------------- 1807594
                                                        item 1-3
   07530-07532 ---------------------------------------------- 1807594
                                                        item 5-7
   07533-07536 ---------------------------------------------- 1807595
   07537 --------------------------------------------------- 1807596
                                                          item 1
   07538 --------------------------------------------------- 1807991
                                                        item 13
   07539-07546 ---------------------------------------------- 1767557
                                                       item 5-12
   07547-07553 ---------------------------------------------- 1767558
                                                        item 1-7
   07554 --------------------------------------------------- 1807992
                                                          item 1
   07555-07556 ---------------------------------------------- 1767558
                                                        item 8-9
   07558-07564 ---------------------------------------------- 1767558
                                                      item 10-16
   07564-07570 ---------------------------------------------- 1767559
                                                        item 1-7
   07571 --------------------------------------------------- 1807483
                                                          item 9
   07572 --------------------------------------------------- 1807594
                                                          item 4
   07572-07575 ---------------------------------------------- 1807484
                                                        item 1-4
   07577-07578 ---------------------------------------------- 1807484
                                                        item 5-6
   07579-07587 ---------------------------------------------- 1807495
   07588-07595 ---------------------------------------------- 1807496
                                                        item 1-8
   07596-07603 ---------------------------------------------- 1809050
                                                        item 2-9
   07606-07610 ---------------------------------------------- 1809050
                                                      item 10-14
   07611-07615 ---------------------------------------------- 1809051
                                                        item 1-3
   07616-07622 ---------------------------------------------- 1809051
                                                       item 4-10
   07623 --------------------------------------------------- 1809051
                                                          item 3
   07624-07629 ---------------------------------------------- 1809051
                                                      item 11-16
   07630-07640 ---------------------------------------------- 1809052
                                                       item 1-11
```

```
07641 ---------------------------------------------------------- 1809198
                                                                 item 16
07642-07653 ---------------------------------------------------- 1809199
07653-07684 ---------------------------------------------------- 1809200
                                                                item 1-16
07686 ----------------------------------------------------------- 1809200
                                                                 item 17
07687-07689 ---------------------------------------------------- 1809201
                                                                 item 1-3
07690-07692 ---------------------------------------------------- 1807596
                                                                 item 2-5
07692-07698 ---------------------------------------------------- 1807597
                                                                 item 1-5
07699-07710 ---------------------------------------------------- 1807597
                                                                item 6-11
07711 [1] ------------------------------------------------------ 1767559
                                                                 item 8
07711 [2] ------------------------------------------------------ 1767560
07711 [3] ------------------------------------------------------ 1767561
                                                                 item 1
07713-07725 ---------------------------------------------------- 1807488
                                                                item 1-13
07727-07731 ---------------------------------------------------- 1807488
                                                               item 14-18
07732-07744 ---------------------------------------------------- 1807489
07745 ----------------------------------------------------------- 1807490
                                                                 item 1
07747-07750 ---------------------------------------------------- 1807598
                                                                 item 1-4
07752-07755 ---------------------------------------------------- 1807598
                                                                 item 5-8
07755 ----------------------------------------------------------- 1807599
07756-07758 ---------------------------------------------------- 1807600
                                                                 item 1-3
07759-07769 ---------------------------------------------------- 1807496
                                                                item 9-18
07770-07785 ---------------------------------------------------- 1807497
07786-07794 ---------------------------------------------------- 1807498
07796 a-k ------------------------------------------------------ 1767561
                                                                 item 2
07796 l-z - 07799 ---------------------------------------------- 1767562
                                                                 item 1-3
07801 ----------------------------------------------------------- 1767562
                                                                 item 4
07803 ----------------------------------------------------------- 1767562
                                                                 item 5
07804-07806 ---------------------------------------------------- 1767563
                                                                 item 1-2
07808-07813 ---------------------------------------------------- 1767563
                                                                 item 3-9
07814-07815 ---------------------------------------------------- 1767564
                                                                 item 1-2
07816-07817 ---------------------------------------------------- 1807561
                                                                 item 7-8
07818-07826 ---------------------------------------------------- 1807562
07827-07830 ---------------------------------------------------- 1807563
                                                                 item 1-4
07832-07837 ---------------------------------------------------- 1807563
                                                                item 5-10
07838-07840 ---------------------------------------------------- 1807564
                                                                 item 1-3
```

```
07841-07846  ------------------------------------------------  1809724
                                                             item 2-7
07847-07852  ------------------------------------------------  1809725
07853-07865  ------------------------------------------------  1809726
07866  ------------------------------------------------------  1809727
                                                             item 1-2
07868-07869  ------------------------------------------------  1809727
                                                             item 3-4
07870  ------------------------------------------------------  1807600
                                                               item 4
07871-07877  ------------------------------------------------  1807601
                                                             item 1-7
07879-07880  ------------------------------------------------  1807601
                                                             item 8-9
07881-07895  ------------------------------------------------  1807602
07895-07905  ------------------------------------------------  1807736
07906-07921  ------------------------------------------------  1809201
                                                            item 8-19
07922-07932  ------------------------------------------------  1809078
07933-07940  ------------------------------------------------  1809323
                                                             item 1-8
07941-07942  ------------------------------------------------  1809052
                                                           item 12-13
07943-07950  ------------------------------------------------  1809053
                                                             item 1-8
07952-07953  ------------------------------------------------  1809053
                                                            item 9-10
07953-07965  ------------------------------------------------  1809054
                                                            item 1-13
07966-07972  ------------------------------------------------  1807490
                                                             item 2-8
07973-07977  ------------------------------------------------  1807491
                                                             item 1-5
07978  ------------------------------------------------------  1807992
                                                               item 2
07979-07986  ------------------------------------------------  1807491
                                                            item 6-13
07987-07990  ------------------------------------------------  1807492
                                                             item 1-4
07992-08000  ------------------------------------------------  1807492
                                                            item 5-13
08001-08013  ------------------------------------------------  1767564
                                                            item 3-15
08013-08022  ------------------------------------------------  1767566
                                                            item 1-10
08024-08026  ------------------------------------------------  1767566
                                                           item 11-13
08028-08029  ------------------------------------------------  1767566
                                                           item 14-15
08030-08039  ------------------------------------------------  1767567
                                                            item 1-10
08040-08047  ------------------------------------------------  1807499
08048-08057  ------------------------------------------------  1807500
                                                            item 1-10
08059-08065  ------------------------------------------------  1807500
                                                           item 11-16
08066-08070  ------------------------------------------------  1807501
                                                             item 1-5
08071-08079  ------------------------------------------------  1807564
                                                            item 4-12
08081-08082  ------------------------------------------------  1807564
                                                           item 13-14
```

```
08083-08090 ------------------------------------------- 1807565
                                                   item 1-8
08092-08094 ------------------------------------------- 1807565
                                                   item 9-11
08095-08101 ------------------------------------------- 1807566
08102-08105 ------------------------------------------- 1807567
                                                   item 1-4
08106 ------------------------------------------------- 1809727
                                                   item 5
08108-08114 ------------------------------------------- 1809727
                                                   item 6-12
08114  (cont.) ----------------------------------------- 1809728
                                                   item 1
08115-08122 ------------------------------------------- 1809728
                                                   item 2-10
08123-08125 ------------------------------------------- 1809729
                                                   item 1-3
08126-08127 ------------------------------------------- 1809054
                                                   item 14-15
08127  (cont.) ----------------------------------------- 1809055
                                                   item 1
08128-08135 ------------------------------------------- 1809055
                                                   item 2-9
08135  (cont.) ----------------------------------------- 1809056
                                                   item 1
08136-08139 ------------------------------------------- 1809056
                                                   item 2-5
08140-08145 ------------------------------------------- 1809037
                                                   item 1-6
08146-08157 ------------------------------------------- 1809323
                                                   item 9-20
08158-08173 ------------------------------------------- 1809324
08174-08180 ------------------------------------------- 1809325
                                                   item 1-7
08181-08187 ------------------------------------------- 1807737
08188-08198 ------------------------------------------- 1807738
                                                   item 1-10
08200-08206 ------------------------------------------- 1807738
                                                   item 11-17
08206-08225 ------------------------------------------- 1807739
08226 ------------------------------------------------- 1807492
                                                   item 14
08227-08241 ------------------------------------------- 1807493
08242-08258 ------------------------------------------- 1807494
08259-08267 ------------------------------------------- 1807584
                                                   item 1-10
08268 ------------------------------------------------- 1807992
                                                   item 3
08269-08273 ------------------------------------------- 1807584
                                                   item 11-16
08276-08277 ------------------------------------------- 1767567
                                                   item 11-12
08277-08292 ------------------------------------------- 1767568
08293-08304 ------------------------------------------- 1767569
08305-08314 ------------------------------------------- 1767570
                                                   item 1-10
08315-08319 ------------------------------------------- 1809729
                                                   item 4-8
08321 ------------------------------------------------- 1809729
                                                   item 9
08323 ------------------------------------------------- 1809729
                                                   item 10
```

```
08324-08325 ------------------------------------------------ 1809730
                                                          item 1-2
08327-08341 ------------------------------------------------ 1809730
                                                          item 3-17
08342 ------------------------------------------------------ 1809731
                                                          item 1
08344-08355 ------------------------------------------------ 1809731
                                                          item 2-14
08356-08368 ------------------------------------------------ 1807501
                                                          item 6-18
08369-08370 ------------------------------------------------ 1807502
                                                          item 1-2
08372-08392 ------------------------------------------------ 1807502
                                                          item 3-12
08393 ------------------------------------------------------ 1807502
                                                          item 13
08394 ------------------------------------------------------ 1807502
                                                          item 12
08395-08396 ------------------------------------------------ 1807502
                                                          item 14-15
08397-08405 ------------------------------------------------ 1807503
                                                          item 1-9
08406-08409 ------------------------------------------------ 1809325
                                                          item 8-12
08410-08423 ------------------------------------------------ 1809326
08424-08430 ------------------------------------------------ 1809327
                                                          item 1-7
08433-08440 ------------------------------------------------ 1809327
                                                          item 8-15
08441-08451/52 --------------------------------------------- 1807740
08451/52-08467 --------------------------------------------- 1807741
08467  (cont.) --------------------------------------------- 1807742
                                                          item 1
08468 ------------------------------------------------------ 1809037
                                                          item 7
08468  (cont.) --------------------------------------------- 1809038
                                                          item 1
08469-08473 ------------------------------------------------ 1809038
                                                          item 2-6
08474 ------------------------------------------------------ 1809039
08474  (cont.) --------------------------------------------- 1809040
                                                          item 1
08475-08478 ------------------------------------------------ 1809040
                                                          item 2-5
08479-08490 ------------------------------------------------ 1807567
                                                          item 5-16
08491-08496 ------------------------------------------------ 1807568
08497-08500 ------------------------------------------------ 1807569
                                                          item 1-4
08501-08504 ------------------------------------------------ 1767570
                                                          item 11-14
08505 ------------------------------------------------------ 1767571
                                                          item 1
08507-08522 ------------------------------------------------ 1767571
                                                          item 2-17
08523-08532 ------------------------------------------------ 1767572
08533-08535 ------------------------------------------------ 1767573
                                                          item 1-3
08536 ------------------------------------------------------ 1807584
                                                          item 17
08538-08549 ------------------------------------------------ 1807585
```

```
08550-08552 ------------------------------------------------- 1807587
                                                         item 1-3
08554-08560 ------------------------------------------------- 1807587
                                                         item 4-10
08561-08567 ------------------------------------------------- 1807742
                                                         item 2-8
08568-08580 ------------------------------------------------- 1807743
                                                         item 1-12
08581 ------------------------------------------------------- 1807992
                                                         item 4
08582-08585 ------------------------------------------------- 1807743
                                                         item 13-16
08586-08595 ------------------------------------------------- 1807744
                                                         item 1-11
08596-08604 ------------------------------------------------- 1809687
08604   (cont.) --------------------------------------------- 1809688
08604-08615 ------------------------------------------------- 1809689
08616-08618 ------------------------------------------------- 1809327
                                                         item 16-18
08619 ------------------------------------------------------- 1809328
                                                         item 1
08620 ------------------------------------------------------- 1807993
                                                         item 1
08621-08641 ------------------------------------------------- 1809328
                                                         item 2-22
08642-08657 ------------------------------------------------- 1809329
08658-08659 ------------------------------------------------- 1809330
                                                         item 1-2
08660-08668 ------------------------------------------------- 1807569
                                                         item 5-13
08669-08672 ------------------------------------------------- 1807551
                                                         item 1-4
08674-08684 ------------------------------------------------- 1807551
                                                         item 5-14
08685 ------------------------------------------------------- 1807552
                                                         item 1
08686-08688 ------------------------------------------------- 1807503
                                                         item 10-12
08689-08705 ------------------------------------------------- 1807504
08706-08716 ------------------------------------------------- 1808482
08717-08720 ------------------------------------------------- 1808483
                                                         item 1-4
08721-08731 ------------------------------------------------- 1809040
                                                         item 6-16
08732-08747 ------------------------------------------------- 1809041
08748-08754 ------------------------------------------------- 1809042
                                                         item 1-7
08755 a-l --------------------------------------------------- 1807744
                                                         item 12
08755 a-l   (cont.) ----------------------------------------- 1807745
                                                         item 1
08755 m-z   (cont.) ----------------------------------------- 1807746
                                                         item 1-2
08755 m-z --------------------------------------------------- 1807745
                                                         item 2
08756-08760 ------------------------------------------------- 1807746
                                                         item 3-7
08761-08765 ------------------------------------------------- 1807747
                                                         item 1-5
08766-08777 ------------------------------------------------- 1767573
                                                         item 4-15
08778-08786 ------------------------------------------------- 1767574
```

```
08787-08790 -------------------------------------------------- 1767575
                                                          item 1-4
08791-08793 a ------------------------------------------- 1807587
                                                        item 11-13
08793-08796 -------------------------------------------------- 1807588
08796-08805 -------------------------------------------------- 1807589
08806-08826 -------------------------------------------------- 1809330
                                                         item 2-23
08827-08834 -------------------------------------------------- 1809400
08838-08846 -------------------------------------------------- 1807747
                                                         item 6-13
08846-08862 -------------------------------------------------- 1807748
08863-08866 -------------------------------------------------- 1807749
                                                          item 1-4
08867-08872 -------------------------------------------------- 1767575
                                                         item 5-10
08873-08885 -------------------------------------------------- 1809543
08886-08893 -------------------------------------------------- 1809544
08894-08898 -------------------------------------------------- 1809545
                                                          item 1-6
08900-08912 -------------------------------------------------- 1809690
08913-08924 -------------------------------------------------- 1809691
08925-08930 -------------------------------------------------- 1809692
                                                          item 1-6
08931-08932 -------------------------------------------------- 1809042
                                                          item 8-9
08934-08936 -------------------------------------------------- 1809042
                                                        item 10-12
08937-08948 -------------------------------------------------- 1809043
08949-08955 -------------------------------------------------- 1809044
                                                          item 1-7
08956-08969 -------------------------------------------------- 1808483
                                                         item 5-17
08970-08986 -------------------------------------------------- 1808484
08987-08990 -------------------------------------------------- 1808485
                                                          item 1-4
08991-08999 -------------------------------------------------- 1807552
                                                         item 2-10
09000 -------------------------------------------------- 1807553
                                                           item 1
09002-09007 -------------------------------------------------- 1807553
                                                          item 2-7
09008-09009 -------------------------------------------------- 1807554
                                                          item 1-2
09011-09015 -------------------------------------------------- 1807554
                                                          item 3-8
09015-09022 -------------------------------------------------- 1809401
                                                          item 1-8
09025-09032 -------------------------------------------------- 1809401
                                                         item 9-16
09034-09039 -------------------------------------------------- 1809401
                                                        item 17-22
09040-09045 -------------------------------------------------- 1809402
                                                          item 1-6
09047-09055 -------------------------------------------------- 1809402
                                                         item 7-15
09056-09059 -------------------------------------------------- 1807590
09060-09069 -------------------------------------------------- 1807591
09069 b -------------------------------------------------- 1807592
                                                           item 1
```

```
09070-09076 ------------------------------------------------ 1809545
                                                        item 7-12
09076  (cont.) ---------------------------------------------- 1809546
                                                        item 1
09077-09089 ------------------------------------------------ 1809546
                                                        item 2-14
09090-09104 ------------------------------------------------ 1809547
                                                        item 1-15
09105-09112 ------------------------------------------------ 1807749
                                                        item 5-11
09117-09125 ------------------------------------------------ 1807750
                                                        item 4-12
09126-09130 ------------------------------------------------ 1807751
                                                        item 1-5
09131 ----------------------------------------------------- 1808485
                                                        item 5
09131  (cont.) ---------------------------------------------- 1808486
                                                        item 1
09132-09142 ------------------------------------------------ 1808486
                                                        item 2-12
09142-09149 ------------------------------------------------ 1809130
                                                        item 2-9
09150-09154 ------------------------------------------------ 1809402
                                                        item 16-20
09155-09160 ------------------------------------------------ 1809403
09161-09165 ------------------------------------------------ 1809404
                                                        item 1-5
09166-09176 ------------------------------------------------ 1807592
                                                        item 2-12
09177-09184 ------------------------------------------------ 1807593
09185 ----------------------------------------------------- 1809044
                                                        item 8
09187 ----------------------------------------------------- 1809044
                                                        item 9
09188-09199 ------------------------------------------------ 1809045
09200-09201 ------------------------------------------------ 1809046
                                                        item 1-2
09202-09210 ------------------------------------------------ 1809692
                                                        item 7-15
09211-09215 ------------------------------------------------ 1809693
09215-09219 ------------------------------------------------ 1809694
                                                        item 1-5
09220 ----------------------------------------------------- 1807751
                                                        item 6
09222-09227 ------------------------------------------------ 1807751
                                                        item 7-12
09228-09232 ------------------------------------------------ 1807752
09233-09251 ------------------------------------------------ 1807753
09252-09254 ------------------------------------------------ 1807754
                                                        item 1-3
09255 a --------------------------------------------------- 1807554
                                                        item 9
09255 b --------------------------------------------------- 1807555
09255 c-92056 --------------------------------------------- 1807556
                                                        item 1-2
09258-09260 ------------------------------------------------ 1807556
                                                        item 3-5
09261-09277 ------------------------------------------------ 1807557
09278-09280 ------------------------------------------------ 1807558
                                                        item 1-3
09281-09283 ------------------------------------------------ 1809130
                                                        item 10-12
```

```
09284-09287 I --------------------------------------------- 1808487
09287 II ------------------------------------------------- 1808488
                                                              item 1
09288-09292 ----------------------------------------------- 1808488
                                                            item 2-6
09293-09295 ----------------------------------------------- 1808489
                                                            item 1-3
09296 ----------------------------------------------------- 1809404
                                                              item 6
09297-09309 ----------------------------------------------- 1809405
09310-09315 ----------------------------------------------- 1809406
                                                            item 1-6
09315 no. 4 ----------------------------------------------- 1809547
                                                             item 16
09315 no. 5-6 --------------------------------------------- 1809548
                                                            item 1-2
09316-09326 ----------------------------------------------- 1809548
                                                           item 3-14
09327-09330 ----------------------------------------------- 1809549
                                                            item 1-6
09331-09336 ----------------------------------------------- 1808019
                                                            item 1-6
09337 ----------------------------------------------------- 1809549
                                                              item 7
09338-09339 ----------------------------------------------- 1808019
                                                            item 7-8
09340 ----------------------------------------------------- 1809549
                                                              item 8
09341 ----------------------------------------------------- 1808019
                                                              item 9
09342-09359 ----------------------------------------------- 1808020
09360 (cont.)-09377 --------------------------------------- 1807755
09378-09389 ----------------------------------------------- 1807792
                                                           item 1-12
09390-09396 ----------------------------------------------- 1809046
                                                            item 3-9
09396 (cont.) --------------------------------------------- 1809143
                                                              item 1
09396 (cont.) --------------------------------------------- 1809142
09397 ----------------------------------------------------- 1809143
                                                              item 2
09397-09399 ----------------------------------------------- 1809144
                                                            item 1-3
09400-09401 ----------------------------------------------- 1809406
                                                            item 7-8
09401 (cont.) --------------------------------------------- 1809407
09401 (cont.) --------------------------------------------- 1809408
                                                              item 1
09402-09407 ----------------------------------------------- 1809408
                                                            item 2-7
09408-09417 ----------------------------------------------- 1808489
                                                           item 4-13
09418-09440 ----------------------------------------------- 1808490
09441-09454 ----------------------------------------------- 1808793
                                                           item 1-14
09455-09464 ----------------------------------------------- 1809550
09465-09470 ----------------------------------------------- 1809551
                                                            item 1-6
09472-09473 ----------------------------------------------- 1809551
                                                            item 7-8
09474-09480 ----------------------------------------------- 1809552
                                                            item 1-7
```

```
09481-09489 ---------------------------------------------------- 1808021
09491-09497 ---------------------------------------------------- 1808022
09498-09500 ---------------------------------------------------- 1808023
                                                            item 1-3
09501-09503 ---------------------------------------------------- 1809694
                                                            item 6-8
09504-09514 ---------------------------------------------------- 1809669
09515-09525 ---------------------------------------------------- 1809670
09526-09527 ---------------------------------------------------- 1807792
                                                          item 13-14
09528-09534 ---------------------------------------------------- 1807793
09535-09542 ---------------------------------------------------- 1807794
09543-09550 ---------------------------------------------------- 1807795
                                                            item 1-8
09551-09555 ---------------------------------------------------- 1809331
09555  (cont.) ------------------------------------------------- 1809332
                                                            item 1
09556-09565 ---------------------------------------------------- 1809332
                                                          item 2-11
09565  (cont.) ------------------------------------------------- 1809332
                                                            item 1
09566 ---------------------------------------------------------- 1809552
                                                            item 8
09568-09570 ---------------------------------------------------- 1809552
                                                          item 9-11
09572-09577 ---------------------------------------------------- 1809552
                                                         item 12-17
09578-09590 ---------------------------------------------------- 1809553
09591-09595 ---------------------------------------------------- 1809554
                                                            item 1-5
09596-09600 ---------------------------------------------------- 1808793
                                                         item 15-19
09602 ---------------------------------------------------------- 1808793
                                                            item 20
09603-09610 ---------------------------------------------------- 1808794
09610  (cont.) ------------------------------------------------- 1808795
                                                            item 1
09611-09612 ---------------------------------------------------- 1807795
                                                          item 9-10
09613-09622 ---------------------------------------------------- 1807796
09623 ---------------------------------------------------------- 1807797
                                                            item 1
09625-09630 ---------------------------------------------------- 1807797
                                                            item 2-7
09631-09634 ---------------------------------------------------- 1809144
                                                            item 4-7
09635-09639 ---------------------------------------------------- 1809145
09640-09658 ---------------------------------------------------- 1809146
09658  (cont.) ------------------------------------------------- 1809147
                                                            item 1
09659-09660 ---------------------------------------------------- 1809147
                                                            item 2-3
09661-09667 ---------------------------------------------------- 1807558
                                                          item 4-10
09668-09674 ---------------------------------------------------- 1807559
                                                            item 1-7
09675-09681 ---------------------------------------------------- 1809333
                                                            item 2-6
09682-09703 ---------------------------------------------------- 1809334
09704-09705 ---------------------------------------------------- 1809335
                                                            item 1-3
```

```
09960      ------------------------------------------------------- 1809672
                                                                       item 16
09961-09970 ------------------------------------------------------ 1809673
09971-09973 ------------------------------------------------------ 1809674
                                                                       item 1-3
09975-09980 ------------------------------------------------------ 1809674
                                                                       item 4-9
09981-09985 ------------------------------------------------------ 1809147
                                                                       item 4-6
09986-09987 ------------------------------------------------------ 1809147
                                                                       item 7-8
09988-09990 ------------------------------------------------------ 1809148
                                                                       item 1-3
09991-09995 ------------------------------------------------------ 1809337
                                                                       item 5-6
09996-10005 ------------------------------------------------------ 1809338
10006-10014 ------------------------------------------------------ 1809339
                                                                       item 1-9
10015-10030 ------------------------------------------------------ 1808799
                                                                       item 3-18
10031-10044 ------------------------------------------------------ 1808800
10045-10046 ------------------------------------------------------ 1808801
                                                                       item 1-2
10048      ------------------------------------------------------- 1809674
                                                                       item 10
10048   (cont.) ------------------------------------------------- 1809675
                                                                       item 1
10049-10060 ------------------------------------------------------ 1809675
                                                                       item 2-13
10061      ------------------------------------------------------- 1809676
                                                                       item 1
10062-10066 ------------------------------------------------------ 1809556
                                                                       item 7-14
10062-10066 ------------------------------------------------------ 1809556
                                                                       item 6-11
10067-10081 ------------------------------------------------------ 1809557
10074 + no. 1 --------------------------------------------------- 1809686
                                                                       item 16
10082-10096 ------------------------------------------------------ 1809558
10097-10099 ------------------------------------------------------ 1809559
                                                                       item 1-3
10100-10105 ------------------------------------------------------ 1808026
                                                                       item 6-11
10116-10118 ------------------------------------------------------ 1809148
                                                                       item 4-6
10119-10123 ------------------------------------------------------ 1809149
10124-10126 ------------------------------------------------------ 1809150
                                                                       item 1-3
10128-10132 ------------------------------------------------------ 1809150
                                                                       item 4-8
10133-10140 ------------------------------------------------------ 1809686
                                                                       item 2-9
10141-10149 ------------------------------------------------------ 1809339
                                                                       item 10-19
10150      ------------------------------------------------------- 1809340
                                                                       item 1-2
10153      ------------------------------------------------------- 1809340
                                                                       item 3
10154-10156 ------------------------------------------------------ 1808801
                                                                       item 3-5
10157      ------------------------------------------------------- 1809340
                                                                       item 4
```

```
10158 ------------------------------------------------ 1808801
                                                         item 6
10160-10166 ---------------------------------------- 1808801
                                                      item 7-13
10167-10176 ---------------------------------------- 1808802
10177 ------------------------------------------------ 1809079
                                                         item 1
10179 ------------------------------------------------ 1809079
                                                         item 2
10180-10184 ---------------------------------------- 1807827
                                                      item 9-13
10185-10189 ---------------------------------------- 1807828
10190-10191 ---------------------------------------- 1807829
                                                      item 1-2
10192 ------------------------------------------------ 1809686
                                                        item 10
10273 ------------------------------------------------ 1809658
                                                         item 9
10196-10197 ---------------------------------------- 1807829
                                                      item 3-4
10198-10202 ---------------------------------------- 1809686
                                                     item 11-15
10203-10205 ---------------------------------------- 1807830
                                                      item 1-3
10207-10208 ---------------------------------------- 1809340
                                                      item 5-6
10209-10213 ---------------------------------------- 1809341
10214-10217 ---------------------------------------- 1809342
                                                      item 1-4
10218-10220 ---------------------------------------- 1809559
                                                      item 4-6
10222-10223 ---------------------------------------- 1809559
                                                         item 7
10224-10227 ---------------------------------------- 1809658
                                                      item 1-4
10228-10229 ---------------------------------------- 1809559
                                                      item 8-9
10229-10233 ---------------------------------------- 1809560
10234-10235 ---------------------------------------- 1809561
                                                      item 1-2
10236-10253 ---------------------------------------- 1808029
                                                     item 2-17
10254-10260 ---------------------------------------- 1808030
                                                      item 1-7
10261-10263 ---------------------------------------- 1809676
                                                      item 2-4
10264-10267 ---------------------------------------- 1809658
                                                      item 5-8
10268-10271 ---------------------------------------- 1809676
                                                      item 5-8
10274-10278 ---------------------------------------- 1809676
                                                     item 9-13
10279-10283 ---------------------------------------- 1809677
10284-10287 ---------------------------------------- 1809678
                                                      item 1-4
10288-10295 ---------------------------------------- 1809079
                                                     item 3-10
10297-10303 ---------------------------------------- 1809079
                                                    item 11-17
10303-10305 ---------------------------------------- 1809080
                                                      item 1-3
```

```
10306-10308 ------------------------------------------------- 1809150
                                                        item 9-11
10309-10313 ------------------------------------------------- 1809151
10314-10315 ------------------------------------------------- 1809069
                                                        item 1-2
10316-10317 ------------------------------------------------- 1809342
                                                        item 5-6
10317  (cont.) --------------------------------------------- 1809343
                                                        item 1
10318 ------------------------------------------------------- 1809343
                                                        item 2
10320-10326 ------------------------------------------------- 1809343
                                                        item 3-9
10326 ------------------------------------------------------- 1809344
                                                        item 1
10327 ------------------------------------------------------- 1809344
                                                        item 2
10327-10338 ------------------------------------------------- 1809561
                                                        item 3-15
10339-10346 ------------------------------------------------- 1809562
                                                        item 1-10
10347-10349 ------------------------------------------------- 1809080
                                                        item 4-6
10350-10358 ------------------------------------------------- 1809081
10358 ------------------------------------------------------- 1807819
10358 ------------------------------------------------------- 1809678
                                                        item 5
10358  (cont.) --------------------------------------------- 1809082
                                                        item 1
10358 ------------------------------------------------------- 1809679
10359-10364 ------------------------------------------------- 1807820
10364  (cont.) --------------------------------------------- 1807821
                                                        item 1
10365-10374 ------------------------------------------------- 1808030
                                                        item 8-12
10374  (cont.) --------------------------------------------- 1808031
                                                        item 1
10375-10382 ------------------------------------------------- 1808031
                                                        item 2-9
10383-10395 ------------------------------------------------- 1808032
10396-10403 ------------------------------------------------- 1808033
10404 ------------------------------------------------------- 1808034
                                                        item 1
10405-10408 ------------------------------------------------- 1809344
                                                        item 3-6
10409 ------------------------------------------------------- 1809345
                                                        item 1
10411-10416 ------------------------------------------------- 1809345
                                                        item 2-7
10417-10422 ------------------------------------------------- 1809069
                                                        item 3-11
10423-10430 ------------------------------------------------- 1809070
10431-10434 ------------------------------------------------- 1809071
                                                        item 1-4
10435-10436 a-k ------------------------------------------- 1807830
                                                        item 4-5
10436 a-k  (cont.) ----------------------------------------- 1807831
                                                        item 1
10436 l-z - 10444 ------------------------------------------ 1807831
                                                        item 2-10
10445-10462 ------------------------------------------------- 1807832
```

```
10459 ---------------------------------------------------- 1809660
                                                            item 2
10463-10469 ---------------------------------------------- 1807833
                                                          item 1-7
10469 ---------------------------------------------------- 1809660
                                                            item 3
10470-10477 ---------------------------------------------- 1809082
                                                         item 2-12
10478-10490 ---------------------------------------------- 1809083
                                                         item 1-14
10491 ---------------------------------------------------- 1809680
10491  (cont.) ------------------------------------------- 1809681
                                                            item 1
10492-10495 ---------------------------------------------- 1809562
                                                        item 11-14
10496-10500 no. 1-2 -------------------------------------- 1809563
10500 ---------------------------------------------------- 1809681
                                                            item 2
10500  (cont.) ------------------------------------------- 1809682
                                                          item 1-3
10500 no. 3-4 -------------------------------------------- 1809564
                                                          item 1-2
10501-10509 ---------------------------------------------- 1809564
                                                          item 3-5
10510-10515 ---------------------------------------------- 1809565
                                                          item 1-6
10516-10525 ---------------------------------------------- 1809660
                                                         item 4-13
10526-10528 ---------------------------------------------- 1809661
                                                          item 1-3
10530 ---------------------------------------------------- 1809661
                                                            item 4
10531-10532 ---------------------------------------------- 1809659
                                                          item 8-9
10533 ---------------------------------------------------- 1809565
                                                            item 7
10534-10536 ---------------------------------------------- 1809659
                                                        item 10-12
10537-10539 ---------------------------------------------- 1809661
                                                          item 5-7
10540 ---------------------------------------------------- 1809659
                                                           item 13
10541 ---------------------------------------------------- 1809660
                                                            item 1
10542-10543 ---------------------------------------------- 1809661
                                                          item 8-9
10544 ---------------------------------------------------- 1809658
                                                           item 10
10545 ---------------------------------------------------- 1809659
                                                            item 7
10546 ---------------------------------------------------- 1809659
                                                            item 6
10547 ---------------------------------------------------- 1809659
                                                            item 5
10548 ---------------------------------------------------- 1809659
                                                            item 4
10549 ---------------------------------------------------- 1809659
                                                            item 3
10550 ---------------------------------------------------- 1809659
                                                            item 2
10551 ---------------------------------------------------- 1809659
                                                            item 1
```

```
10552    ------------------------------------------------------------ 1809658
                                                                        item 11
10553-10556  ------------------------------------------------------ 1807821
                                                                        item 2-5
10557-10560  ------------------------------------------------------ 1807822
10561-10568  ------------------------------------------------------ 1807823
10569-10570  ------------------------------------------------------ 1807824
                                                                        item 1-2
10571-10575  ------------------------------------------------------ 1809682
                                                                        item 4-8
10576-10577  ------------------------------------------------------ 1809683
                                                                        item 2-3
10579-10588  ------------------------------------------------------ 1809683
                                                                        item 4-13
10585    (cont.)  ------------------------------------------------- 1809566
                                                                        item 1
10588    (cont.)  ------------------------------------------------- 1809684
                                                                        item 1
10589-10590  ------------------------------------------------------ 1809684
                                                                        item 2-3
10591-10602  ------------------------------------------------------ 1809346
                                                                        item 1-12
10603    ------------------------------------------------------------ 1808034
                                                                        item 2
10603    (cont.)  ------------------------------------------------- 1808035
10603    (cont.)  ------------------------------------------------- 1808036
                                                                        item 1
10604-10614  ------------------------------------------------------ 1809566
                                                                        item 2-12
10615-10627  ------------------------------------------------------ 1809567
10628    ------------------------------------------------------------ 1809346
                                                                        item 13
10628-10636  ------------------------------------------------------ 1809347
10637-10640  ------------------------------------------------------ 1809348
10641    ------------------------------------------------------------ 1809349
                                                                        item 1
10643-10644  ------------------------------------------------------ 1809083
                                                                        item 15-16
10645-10650  ------------------------------------------------------ 1809084
10651-10653  ------------------------------------------------------ 1809085
                                                                        item 1-4
10654-10656  ------------------------------------------------------ 1809071
                                                                        item 5-9
10656    (cont.)  ------------------------------------------------- 1809072
                                                                        item 1
10657-10674  ------------------------------------------------------ 1809072
                                                                        item 2-19
10674    (cont.)  ------------------------------------------------- 1809073
                                                                        item 1
10675-10680  ------------------------------------------------------ 1808036
                                                                        item 2-7
10680-10684  ------------------------------------------------------ 1808037
                                                                        item 1-6
10685-10691  ------------------------------------------------------ 1809661
                                                                        item 10-16
10692-10700  ------------------------------------------------------ 1809662
                                                                        item 1-9
10701-10706  ------------------------------------------------------ 1808037
                                                                        item 7-12
10707    ------------------------------------------------------------ 1807824
                                                                        item 3
```

```
10707  (cont.) -------------------------------------------- 1807825
                                                             item 1
10708-10716 --------------------------------------------- 1807825
                                                           item 2-10
10717-10720 --------------------------------------------- 1808000
                                                           item 1-4
10721-10724 --------------------------------------------- 1809684
                                                           item 4-7
10725 --------------------------------------------------- 1809683
                                                           item 1
10725  (cont.) -------------------------------------------- 1809685
                                                           item 1
10726-10730 --------------------------------------------- 1809685
                                                           item 2-6
10730-10736 --------------------------------------------- 1809349
                                                           item 2-8
10736  (cont.) -------------------------------------------- 1809350
                                                           item 1
10737-10743 --------------------------------------------- 1809350
                                                           item 2-8
10744-10752 --------------------------------------------- 1809662
                                                          item 10-18
10753 --------------------------------------------------- 1809663
                                                           item 2
10754 --------------------------------------------------- 1809663
                                                           item 1
10755-10766 --------------------------------------------- 1809663
                                                          item 3-14
10767-10769 --------------------------------------------- 1809350
                                                          item 9-11
10770-10773 --------------------------------------------- 1808000
                                                           item 5-8
10774 --------------------------------------------------- 1807993
                                                           item 2-3
10775 --------------------------------------------------- 1808000
                                                           item 9
10777 --------------------------------------------------- 1808000
                                                           item 10
10778-10780 --------------------------------------------- 1808001
                                                           item 1-3
10781 --------------------------------------------------- 1808037
                                                           item 13
10781  (cont.) -------------------------------------------- 1808143
                                                           item 1
10782-10787 --------------------------------------------- 1808143
                                                           item 2-8
10789-10790 --------------------------------------------- 1808143
                                                          item 9-11
10791-10800 --------------------------------------------- 1809664
                                                          item 1-10
10801-10803 --------------------------------------------- 1808144
                                                           item 1-3
10804 --------------------------------------------------- 1809664
                                                           item 11
10805-10807 --------------------------------------------- 1808144
                                                           item 4-6
10808-10813 --------------------------------------------- 1809350
                                                          item 12-17
10814-10825 --------------------------------------------- 1809351
10826-10828 --------------------------------------------- 1809352
                                                           item 1-3
```

```
10829 --------------------------------------------------------- 1809073
                                                                   item 2
10830-10832 ---------------------------------------------------- 1809074
                                                                 item 1-3
10833-10840 ---------------------------------------------------- 1808001
                                                                item 4-11
10841-10851 ---------------------------------------------------- 1808002
10852-10860 ---------------------------------------------------- 1809568
10860-10865 ---------------------------------------------------- 1809569
                                                                 item 1-6
10866 --------------------------------------------------------- 1809085
                                                                   item 5
10867-10868 ---------------------------------------------------- 1809086
                                                                 item 1-2
10870-10882 ---------------------------------------------------- 1809086
                                                                item 3-16
10882  (cont.) ----------------------------------------------- 1809087
                                                                   item 1
10883-10886 ---------------------------------------------------- 1809087
                                                                 item 2-5
10887-10897 ---------------------------------------------------- 1807833
                                                                item 8-18
10898-10910 ---------------------------------------------------- 1807834
                                                                item 1-13
10911-10912 ---------------------------------------------------- 1809074
                                                                 item 4-6
10912  (cont.) ----------------------------------------------- 1809075
                                                                   item 1
10913-10920 ---------------------------------------------------- 1809075
                                                                 item 2-9
10922-10924 ---------------------------------------------------- 1809075
                                                               item 10-12
10925 --------------------------------------------------------- 1809076
                                                                   item 1
10926-10930 ---------------------------------------------------- 1809352
                                                                 item 4-8
10931 --------------------------------------------------------- 1809076
                                                                   item 2
10932-10933 ---------------------------------------------------- 1809352
                                                                item 9-10
10934-10947 ---------------------------------------------------- 1809353
10948 --------------------------------------------------------- 1809354
                                                                   item 1
10949-10955 ---------------------------------------------------- 1809569
                                                                item 7-13
10956-10962 no. 1 ---------------------------------------------- 1809570
10962 no. 1  (cont.) ------------------------------------------- 1809571
                                                                   item 1
10962 no. 2 --------------------------------------------------- 1809571
                                                                   item 2
10963-10965 ---------------------------------------------------- 1809571
                                                                 item 3-5
10966-10971 ---------------------------------------------------- 1808144
                                                                item 7-12
10971-10982 ---------------------------------------------------- 1808145
10994-11008 ---------------------------------------------------- 1807985
11009-11015 ---------------------------------------------------- 1807986
                                                                 item 1-9
11016-11021 ---------------------------------------------------- 1809087
                                                                item 6-11
11022-11038 --------------------------------------------------- 1809124
```

```
11039-11045 ------------------------------------------------------ 1809354
                                                           item 2-8
11046-11055 ------------------------------------------------------ 1809355
                                                           item 1-10
11056-11059 ------------------------------------------------------ 1807834
                                                           item 14-17
11060-11067 ------------------------------------------------------ 1808006
                                                           item 1-8
11068-11069 ------------------------------------------------------ 1809355
                                                           item 11-12
11070-11074 ------------------------------------------------------ 1808006
                                                           item 9-14
11076-11077 ------------------------------------------------------ 1809355
                                                           item 13-14
11083 ------------------------------------------------------------ 1807990
                                                           item 1-3
11085 ------------------------------------------------------------ 1807990
                                                           item 4
11086-11090 ------------------------------------------------------ 1809125
                                                           item 1-5
11091 ------------------------------------------------------------ 1808007
                                                           item 1
11092-11093 ------------------------------------------------------ 1809125
                                                           item 6-7
11094 ------------------------------------------------------------ 1808148
                                                           item 3
11095-11096 ------------------------------------------------------ 1809125
                                                           item 8-9
11097 ------------------------------------------------------------ 1808149
                                                           item 10
11098 ------------------------------------------------------------ 1809067
                                                           item 4
11099 ------------------------------------------------------------ 1809125
                                                           item 10
11100 ------------------------------------------------------------ 1807990
                                                           item 5-6
11101 ------------------------------------------------------------ 1808146
                                                           item 1
11104 ------------------------------------------------------------ 1807990
                                                           item 7
11104   (cont.) ---------------------------------------------------- 1807991
                                                           item 1
11105 ------------------------------------------------------------ 1808146
                                                           item 2
11106 ------------------------------------------------------------ 1809067
                                                           item 5
11107-11111 ------------------------------------------------------ 1808146
                                                           item 3-7
11112 ------------------------------------------------------------ 1809067
                                                           item 6
11113-11114 ------------------------------------------------------ 1808146
                                                           item 8-9
11114-11115 ------------------------------------------------------ 1807991
                                                           item 2-3
11116 ------------------------------------------------------------ 1808146
                                                           item 10
11117-11125 ------------------------------------------------------ 1807991
                                                           item 4-12
11126 ------------------------------------------------------------ 1807986
                                                           item 10
11127-11129 ------------------------------------------------------ 1809127
                                                           item 2-4
```

```
11131-11132 --------------------------------------------------- 1807986
                                                        item 11-12
11133 --------------------------------------------------------- 1808150
                                                        item 1-2
11134 --------------------------------------------------------- 1807993
                                                        item 4
11134-11138 --------------------------------------------------- 1809127
                                                        item 5-10
11139 --------------------------------------------------------- 1807987
                                                        item 1
11140-11142 --------------------------------------------------- 1809127
                                                        item 11-14
11143-11145 --------------------------------------------------- 1807987
                                                        item 2-4
11146 --------------------------------------------------------- 1809128
                                                        item 19
11147-11149 --------------------------------------------------- 1809685
                                                        item 7-9
11150-11151 --------------------------------------------------- 1809356
                                                        item 14-15
11152 --------------------------------------------------------- 1809685
                                                        item 10
11154-11156 --------------------------------------------------- 1809685
                                                        item 11-13
11157 --------------------------------------------------------- 1809356
                                                        item 16
11158 --------------------------------------------------------- 1809685
                                                        item 14
11159-11160 --------------------------------------------------- 1809356
                                                        item 17-18
11161-11163 --------------------------------------------------- 1809357
                                                        item 1-3
11164 --------------------------------------------------------- 1809686
                                                        item 1
11165-11168 --------------------------------------------------- 1809357
                                                        item 4-7
11169 --------------------------------------------------------- 1809128
                                                        item 1
11170 --------------------------------------------------------- 1809128
                                                        item 20
11170   (cont.) ----------------------------------------------- 1809129
                                                        item 1-2
11171-11176 --------------------------------------------------- 1809128
                                                        item 2-7
11177 --------------------------------------------------------- 1808148
                                                        item 4
11178-11180 --------------------------------------------------- 1809128
                                                        item 8-10
11181 --------------------------------------------------------- 1808150
                                                        item 3-4
11182 --------------------------------------------------------- 1808148
                                                        item 5
11183-11187 --------------------------------------------------- 1809128
                                                        item 11-15
11188 --------------------------------------------------------- 1808148
                                                        item 6
11189 --------------------------------------------------------- 1809128
                                                        item 16
11190-11192 --------------------------------------------------- 1808148
                                                        item 7-9
11193-11194 --------------------------------------------------- 1809128
                                                        item 17-18
```

```
11195 ------------------------------------------------------- 1808148
                                                         item 10
11196 ------------------------------------------------------- 1808150
                                                          item 5
11197-11199 ------------------------------------------------- 1809067
                                                         item 7-9
11200 ------------------------------------------------------- 1808150
                                                          item 6
11201-11203 ------------------------------------------------- 1808146
                                                        item 11-13
11204 ------------------------------------------------------- 1808148
                                                         item 11
11205 ------------------------------------------------------- 1808146
                                                         item 14
11206 ------------------------------------------------------- 1808147
                                                          item 1
11207 ------------------------------------------------------- 1809067
                                                         item 10
11208 ------------------------------------------------------- 1808147
                                                          item 2
11209 ------------------------------------------------------- 1809067
                                                         item 11
11210-11211 ------------------------------------------------- 1808147
                                                         item 3-4
11212 ------------------------------------------------------- 1809067
                                                         item 12
11213 ------------------------------------------------------- 1808147
                                                          item 5
11214 ------------------------------------------------------- 1809067
                                                         item 13
11215 ------------------------------------------------------- 1807987
                                                          item 9
11217 ------------------------------------------------------- 1809067
                                                         item 14
11218-11219 ------------------------------------------------- 1808007
                                                         item 2-3
11220 ------------------------------------------------------- 1809067
                                                         item 15
11221 ------------------------------------------------------- 1808151
                                                          item 1
11221-11224 ------------------------------------------------- 1808007
                                                        item 4-10
11225 ------------------------------------------------------- 1809068
                                                          item 1
11226 ------------------------------------------------------- 1808007
                                                         item 11
11227 ------------------------------------------------------- 1809068
                                                          item 2
11228-11230 ------------------------------------------------- 1809068
                                                         item 3-5
11232 ------------------------------------------------------- 1807987
                                                          item 5
11233-11240 ------------------------------------------------- 1809068
                                                        item 6-12
11241 ------------------------------------------------------- 1808007
                                                         item 12
11242 ------------------------------------------------------- 1809068
                                                         item 13
11243 ------------------------------------------------------- 1808007
                                                         item 13
11244 ------------------------------------------------------- 1809068
                                                         item 14
```

```
11245 ------------------------------------------------------------- 1808007
                                                                  item 14
11246 ------------------------------------------------------------- 1809068
                                                                  item 15
11247 ------------------------------------------------------------- 1809355
                                                                  item 15
11248 ------------------------------------------------------------- 1808148
                                                                  item 12
11249-11250 ------------------------------------------------------- 1809355
                                                                item 16-17
11251 ------------------------------------------------------------- 1808007
                                                                  item 15
11252-11254 ------------------------------------------------------- 1807987
                                                                 item 6-8
11255 ------------------------------------------------------------- 1809355
                                                                  item 18
11256 ------------------------------------------------------------- 1807993
                                                                   item 5
11257 ------------------------------------------------------------- 1808008
                                                                   item 1
11258-11262 ------------------------------------------------------- 1809355
                                                                item 19-23
11263 ------------------------------------------------------------- 1808008
                                                                   item 2
11264-11266 ------------------------------------------------------- 1809355
                                                                item 24-26
11267-11269 ------------------------------------------------------- 1808008
                                                                 item 3-5
11269-11271 ------------------------------------------------------- 1809355
                                                                item 27-29
11272-11275 ------------------------------------------------------- 1809356
                                                                 item 1-4
11276-11278 ------------------------------------------------------- 1808008
                                                                 item 6-8
11279 ------------------------------------------------------------- 1809357
                                                                   item 8
11280 ------------------------------------------------------------- 1808148
                                                                  item 13
11282 ------------------------------------------------------------- 1807987
                                                                item 10-11
11283 ------------------------------------------------------------- 1809356
                                                                   item 5
11284 ------------------------------------------------------------- 1808149
                                                                   item 1
11285 ------------------------------------------------------------- 1809356
                                                                   item 6
11286 ------------------------------------------------------------- 1808149
                                                                   item 2
11287 ------------------------------------------------------------- 1809356
                                                                   item 7
11288-11289 ------------------------------------------------------- 1808149
                                                                 item 3-4
11290 ------------------------------------------------------------- 1808008
                                                                   item 9
11291-11229 ------------------------------------------------------- 1808149
                                                                 item 5-6
11292 ------------------------------------------------------------- 1809076
                                                                   item 3
11293 ------------------------------------------------------------- 1809129
                                                                   item 3
11294 ------------------------------------------------------------- 1809356
                                                                   item 8
```

129

```
11295 --------------------------------------------------- 1808151
                                                          item 2
11297 --------------------------------------------------- 1809076
                                                          item 4
11298 --------------------------------------------------- 1808149
                                                          item 7
11299-11300 --------------------------------------------- 1809076
                                                          item 5-6
11301-11303 --------------------------------------------- 1809077
                                                          item 1-3
11304 --------------------------------------------------- 1809356
                                                          item 9
11305-11309 --------------------------------------------- 1809077
                                                          item 4-8
11310 --------------------------------------------------- 1809357
                                                          item 9
11311 --------------------------------------------------- 1809356
                                                          item 10
11312 --------------------------------------------------- 1809357
                                                          item 10
11312-11313 --------------------------------------------- 1809077
                                                          item 9-10
11314 --------------------------------------------------- 1809357
                                                          item 11
11315 --------------------------------------------------- 1807987
                                                          item 12
11316-11317 --------------------------------------------- 1809357
                                                          item 12-13
11318 --------------------------------------------------- 1809077
                                                          item 11
11319-11320 --------------------------------------------- 1809356
                                                          item 11-12
11321-11322 --------------------------------------------- 1808149
                                                          item 8-9
11323-11329 --------------------------------------------- 1808147
                                                          item 6-12
11330-11331 --------------------------------------------- 1808148
                                                          item 1-2
11332-11334 --------------------------------------------- 1809077
                                                          item 12-14
11334   (cont.) --------------------------------------- 1809067
                                                          item 1
11335-11336 --------------------------------------------- 1807988
11337-11338 --------------------------------------------- 1809129
                                                          item 4-5
11338   (cont.) --------------------------------------- 1809130
                                                          item 1
11339 --------------------------------------------------- 1809356
                                                          item 13
11340 --------------------------------------------------- 1809067
                                                          item 2
11341-11344 --------------------------------------------- 1807989
11346 --------------------------------------------------- 1809125
                                                          item 11
11346 --------------------------------------------------- 1809126
11346 --------------------------------------------------- 1809127
                                                          item 1
11347 --------------------------------------------------- 1809357
                                                          item 14
11348 --------------------------------------------------- 1809067
                                                          item 3
```

```
11349-11350 ---------------------------------------------- 1809357
                                                          item 15-16
11351-11352 ---------------------------------------------- 1809358
                                                          item 1-2
11355-11360 ---------------------------------------------- 1809358
                                                          item 3-8
F. 00024 ------------------------------------------------- 1809667
F. 00033 ------------------------------------------------- 1809667
F. 00076 ------------------------------------------------- 1809667
F. 00112 ------------------------------------------------- 1809667
F. 00117 ------------------------------------------------- 1809667
F. 00126 ------------------------------------------------- 1809667
F. 00184-00185 ------------------------------------------- 1809667
F. 00208 ------------------------------------------------- 1809667
F. 00217-00218 ------------------------------------------- 1809667
F. 00222 ------------------------------------------------- 1809667
F. 00232-00233 ------------------------------------------- 1809667
F. 00242 ------------------------------------------------- 1809668
F. 00245 ------------------------------------------------- 1809668
F. 00501 ------------------------------------------------- 1809668
F. 00508 ------------------------------------------------- 1809668
F. 00513 ------------------------------------------------- 1809668
F. 00522-00523 ------------------------------------------- 1809668
F. 00525 ------------------------------------------------- 1809668
F. 00527-00528 ------------------------------------------- 1809668
F. 00530 ------------------------------------------------- 1809668
F. 00532 ------------------------------------------------- 1809668
F. 00539-00541 ------------------------------------------- 1809668
F. 00543 ------------------------------------------------- 1809668
F. 00545 ------------------------------------------------- 1809668
F. 00550 ------------------------------------------------- 1809668
F. 00557-00558 ------------------------------------------- 1809668
F. 00561 ------------------------------------------------- 1809668
F. 00563 ------------------------------------------------- 1809668
N. 00183-00186 ------------------------------------------- 1809538
N. 00188 ------------------------------------------------- 1809538
N. 00190 ------------------------------------------------- 1809538
N. 00194 ------------------------------------------------- 1809538
N. 00196-00199 ------------------------------------------- 1809538
N. 00199-00202 ------------------------------------------- 1809538
N. 00204-00205 ------------------------------------------- 1809538
N. 00207 ------------------------------------------------- 1809538
N. 00209-00217 ------------------------------------------- 1809538
N. 00220-00228 ------------------------------------------- 1809538
N. 00229-00236 ------------------------------------------- 1809539
N. 00238 ------------------------------------------------- 1809539
N. 00240-00244 ------------------------------------------- 1809538
N. 00248 ------------------------------------------------- 1809539
N. 00249 ------------------------------------------------- 1809539
N. 00251-00252 ------------------------------------------- 1809539
N. 00254-00255 ------------------------------------------- 1809539
N. 00257 ------------------------------------------------- 1809539
N. 00259-00261 ------------------------------------------- 1809539
N. 00262 ------------------------------------------------- 1809539
N. 00264 ------------------------------------------------- 1809539
N. 00266-00269 ------------------------------------------- 1809539
N. 00275-00285 ------------------------------------------- 1809539
N. 00286-00288 ------------------------------------------- 1809665
N. 00290 ------------------------------------------------- 1809665
N. 00292-00297 ------------------------------------------- 1809665
N. 00299-00309 ------------------------------------------- 1809665
N. 00311-00314 ------------------------------------------- 1809665
```

```
N. 00316-00317 -------------------------------------------------- 1809665
N. 00319-00321 -------------------------------------------------- 1809665
N. 00329-00335 -------------------------------------------------- 1809665
N. 00338-00346 -------------------------------------------------- 1809665
N. 00347 -------------------------------------------------------- 1809666
N. 00350-00357 -------------------------------------------------- 1809666
N. 00358 -------------------------------------------------------- 1808003
N. 00358-00375 -------------------------------------------------- 1808003
N. 00376 -------------------------------------------------------- 1809539
N. 00379-00380 -------------------------------------------------- 1808003
N. 00382 -------------------------------------------------------- 1808003
N. 00384-00389 -------------------------------------------------- 1808003
N. 00390-00395 -------------------------------------------------- 1808004
N. 00397-00409 -------------------------------------------------- 1808004
N. 00410 -------------------------------------------------------- 1809539
N. 00412-00414 -------------------------------------------------- 1809539
N. 00416-00424 -------------------------------------------------- 1809539
N. 00426-00429 -------------------------------------------------- 1809539
N. 00433-00435 -------------------------------------------------- 1809539
N. 00436-00448 -------------------------------------------------- 1809540
N. 00449 -------------------------------------------------------- 1809541
N. 00504 -------------------------------------------------------- 1809539
N. 00534-00541 -------------------------------------------------- 1809666
N. 00543 -------------------------------------------------------- 1809666
N. 00546-00549 -------------------------------------------------- 1809666
N. 00551-00552 -------------------------------------------------- 1809666
N. 00553 -------------------------------------------------------- 1809665
N. 00554 -------------------------------------------------------- 1809666
N. 00556-00557 -------------------------------------------------- 1809666
N. 00559-00560 -------------------------------------------------- 1809666
N. 00562-00565 -------------------------------------------------- 1809666
N. 00566-00572 -------------------------------------------------- 1809667
N. 00574-00579 -------------------------------------------------- 1809667
N. 00580 -------------------------------------------------------- 1809666
N. 00581-00584 -------------------------------------------------- 1809667
N. 00587-00589 -------------------------------------------------- 1809667
N. 00592 -------------------------------------------------------- 1809667
N. 00594-00595 -------------------------------------------------- 1809667
N. 00785 -------------------------------------------------------- 1809541
N. 00789 -------------------------------------------------------- 1809541
N. 00800-00801 -------------------------------------------------- 1809541
N. 00809 -------------------------------------------------------- 1809541
N. 00838-00839 -------------------------------------------------- 1809541
N. 00841-00844 -------------------------------------------------- 1809541
N. 00846 -------------------------------------------------------- 1809541
N. 00850 -------------------------------------------------------- 1809541
N. 00870 -------------------------------------------------------- 1809541
N. 00872-00881 -------------------------------------------------- 1809541
N. 00891 -------------------------------------------------------- 1809541
N. 00896 -------------------------------------------------------- 1809541
N. 00904-00908 -------------------------------------------------- 1809541
N. 00923-00924 -------------------------------------------------- 1809541
N. 00926-00930 -------------------------------------------------- 1809541
N. 00932-00935 -------------------------------------------------- 1809541
N. 00945 -------------------------------------------------------- 1809542
                                                                  item 1
N. 01360 -------------------------------------------------------- 1808004
N. 01360  (cont.) ----------------------------------------------- 1808005
N. 01361 -------------------------------------------------------- 1808005
N. 01365-01370 -------------------------------------------------- 1808005
N. 01380-01383 -------------------------------------------------- 1808005
N. 01385-01386 -------------------------------------------------- 1808005
```

```
N.  01388 ---------------------------------------------- 1808005
N.  01398 ---------------------------------------------- 1808005
N.  01408 ---------------------------------------------- 1808005
N.  01541 ---------------------------------------------- 1808005
N.  01552 ---------------------------------------------- 1808005
N.  01559 ---------------------------------------------- 1808004
N.  01561-01562 ----------------------------------------- 1808005
N.  01688 ---------------------------------------------- 1808005
N.  01693-01695 ----------------------------------------- 1808005
Z.  00001-00064 ----------------------------------------- 1809542
                                                          item 1
Z.  00065-00098 ----------------------------------------- 1809542
                                                          item 2
```